To Do List

How to Increase Your Productivity and Master Your Time

(An Easy to Use to Do List Formula to Save Hours of Your Time)

Richard Dixon

Published By **John Kembrey**

Richard Dixon

To Do List: How to Increase Your Productivity and Master Your Time (An Easy to Use to Do List Formula to Save Hours of Your Time)

ISBN   978-1-998927-24-1

No part of this guidebook shall be reproduced in any form without permission in writing from the publisher except in the case of brief quotations embodied in critical articles or reviews.

Legal & Disclaimer

The information contained in this book is not designed to replace or take the place of any form of medicine or professional medical advice. The information in this book has been provided for educational & entertainment purposes only.

The information contained in this book has been compiled from sources deemed reliable, and it is accurate to the best of the Author's knowledge; however, the Author cannot guarantee its accuracy and validity and cannot be held liable for any errors or omissions. Changes are periodically made to this book. You must consult your doctor or get professional medical advice before using any of the suggested remedies, techniques, or information in this book.

Table Of Contents

Chapter 1: All About The To-Do List

Before we get into the intricacies of a To-Do listing, allow me first introduce you to this situation be counted with a bit statistics – What is a To-Do listing? What forms of To-Do listing do people commonly create? What is a improper To-Do listing?

What is a To-Do List?

Do you regularly experience deluged through the sheer multitude of duties in your plate? Do you discover it hard to satisfy time limits? Or do essential matters slip out of your thoughts? All of those are signs of now not preserving a properly-drafted "To-Do listing."

To-Do Lists are prioritized lists of all the duties which you want to get completed. They listing the entirety you have to undertake and get finished, with the maximum great obligations on the top, and the secondary responsibilities at the lowest of the list.

A To-Do listing ensures that your obligations are all listed in a single region so you don't neglect some aspect and you will be able to meet your deadlines resultseasily. It is critical to have a To-Do list if you are overloaded with obligations. It is the splendid and most effective tool for green time manage.

A To-Do listing may be divided into 4 differing types. Let's study those in element below:

Introducing Different Types of To-Do Lists

In the advent, I cited that some human beings take a hasty method to their lists. They upload mind, emergencies and tertiary responsibilities all onto the same list, which makes it hard to behave upon. As a prevent end result, this frequently makes their To-Do listing absolutely unproductive.

In order to growth productivity, we want to genuinely define the sports activities that make up our days, weeks and months. One solution I identified is to create and preserve 4 types of To-Do lists - every serving a unique varieties of paintings.

Here are the terrific forms of lists:

1. The Idea List – This is used because the treasure box for each idea that comes for your thoughts. Some of these mind may be performed, at the equal time as others might not be. However, the primary cause of this list is to build up lots of thoughts; who is aware of, one can also end up our existence-saver sooner or later. Update on a every day foundation and evaluation it at least as soon as consistent with week.

2. The Every Week Task List – Every week comes with tremendous task cut-off dates

and scheduled appointments. Each week is a combination of each expert and personal responsibilities that want to be fulfilled on a sure day at a selected time. So earlier than you start getting equipped for the imminent week, make a be conscious on this listing of the obligations that need to be finished within the week in advance. This listing will embody things like undertaking duties, private appointments together with beauty or health check-ups, weekly purchaser calls and conferences.

three. The Project List − If a task or assignment requires greater than separate movements, the challenge listing comes into the image. This form of listing typically acts as a bridge maximum of the idea-era degree and the assignment-final contact degree.

four. The Urgent Task List (UTL) − As the call implies, this listing includes of the maximum important matters that want to be executed. The UTL is a small list of obligations which might be your top priority for that day. The maximum essential purpose of this sort of list is to finish the ones items in advance than performing some thing else. For example, maximum human beings check their private emails and Facebook account within the first hour in their day. With this listing, you'll adopt small important responsibilities indexed in the UTL first, as quick as you get to the workplace.

Apart from the above list types, you may additionally have four unique sub-lists in the important listing. This includes (http://wearelikeminds.Com/):

● Next List – This is the list in which you'll listing your next tangible and measurable actions.

● Project List – Here you'll list responsibilities already in your plate.

• Someday List – This consists of gadgets that you need to do in the future that don't continuously require a very last date.

• Waiting List – As the call implies, this is composed of factors which you are ready to pay attention about from someone to whom you assigned a selected venture.

Now you may feel that growing and keeping 4 absolutely certainly one of a kind lists for one-of-a-type duties might be time-consuming and may emerge as difficult. You can also ask your self, why need to I spend my precious time in growing four specific types of lists? The answer is simple. Because doing this could assist you in reality define your goals, it's going to help with effective time manipulate and assist you in focusing the most power on your most important duties.

Despite know-how the significance of a growing a To-Do list and approaches of making a efficient list, people however dedicate mistakes and emerge as drafting incorrect To-Do list. Here's a traditional example of a incorrect listing.

A Flawed To-Do List

A incorrect list is one that isn't been described surely and is a long way too subjective to be done. Check out the easy instance of a incorrect To-Do listing:

● Write an in depth preserve evaluation for the newly-opened splendor store, nowadays.

● Need to go away at 7:10-7:15 for film — or at the ultra-present day-day via 7:45 p.M.

● Write and end autobiography these days.

- Clean my face with water or milk cleanser to cast off pimples.

This To-Do list is flawed in many methods. Some devices are too considerable to be finished in one strive like writing an autobiography, on the equal time as the alternative one is actually a suggestion for zits elimination. The dreams are not definitely described right right here.

In the imminent chapters you'll discover ways to create a listing and what errors to keep away from at the same time as drafting one.

Chapter 2: Are You Feeling Burdened?

I guess you are analyzing this e-book due to the fact you are weighed down – each a chunk or masses. Possibly you enjoy that the every day amount of emails for your mailbox is growing and it slow to take a look at them is decreasing. If I'm now not incorrect, you're even feeling unproductive in recent times, right? Or perhaps you feeling your strolling hours are really out of manage – your actual paintings is getting swallowed below perpetual emergencies. Are you going via any of the above troubles? Wonderful!

No, I'm now not joking! I said "first rate" because of the fact on this ebook you'll come across many amazingly drafted brief fixes at the manner to make your lifestyles less difficult and responsibilities effortlessly capacity. At the give up of every bankruptcy you'll find a way on your problem, or an expertise of what you need to expect and what to do for max usage of the time you have got were given have been given to be had.

If you're feeling overloaded, don't worry. Nearly everybody nowadays faces this hassle. In truth, most human beings in my expert and personal address-ebook say they are now not glad with their jobs and are looking for a few thing new. When requested the purpose, they may be saying that they may be sick-used – that they have too much work, at the identical time as the amount of time they should accomplish the art work internal stays the identical.

Guys, there's an answer – get a To-Do listing!

Tens of lots of human beings have skilled a extremely good change of their walking sample through using To-Do lists. With the assist of a To-Do listing you can see your priorities in reality and might master them. Additionally, running from a list enables lessen pressure. However you want to be careful to make sure your listing is properly-planned and correctly created.

Still not glad? In the subsequent financial ruin, you'll discover more clear and sensible reasons for developing a To-Do list.

Chapter 3: Why Most Of Us Create A To-Do List?

The essential but most important question is, why will we need to install writing down a To-Do listing? Most people reply that it acts as a prompt to help us don't forget essential responsibilities.

We frequently pay attention human beings say, "if I don't write it down, I'll forget some component essential," and they hurriedly scribble a notice to maintain XYZ gadgets from grocery shops, go to financial corporation for account-associated enquiry at 11:00 a.M. Or take Mom for a ordinary fitness check-up on Monday at four p.M. We hold a examine of most of these responsibilities, announcing it's far "crucial."

Surprisingly, if it's a really urgent mission, preferably it should stick in your mind. In fact, maximum humans are capable of preserving some of tremendous obligations in our head at any given time period. We seldom neglect those gadgets which might be of maximum significance. Despite this, maximum people be conscious it of their listing for masses of motives.

For some, it becomes without a doubt tough to remember subjects on time. While for others, writing brings a experience of rest and assist, because of the reality we understand that if the next day morning our mind stops running, we're capable of continually be guided thru our To-Do listing. But this can bring about humans getting burdened about compiling a To-Do list.

I sincerely have a journalist inner me! I found out this on the equal time as I end up sketching an define for this ebook. I were given an idea – why not ask human beings round me for reasons why they select developing a To-Do listing. When I inquired, I were given an entire lot of reasons, a number of which have been genuinely unexpected.

My adolescence buddy said "it orders my lifestyles."

Although the range is small, a few humans jot down subjects in their To-Do list that have no viable threat of being completed in the time decided thru them. Such lists commonly fail to preserve the stableness people count on from them. Obviously then, we need to refrain from developing those sort of such lists.

In my research to discover why people list matters, I additionally decided folks who stated listing is fairly clean and greater gratifying than writing. It is an superb way to warmth up your thoughts cells to put together your mind to paintings towards accomplishment of the listed obligations.

When it comes to my very personal technique, I experience really uneasy searching at pending responsibilities in competition to my call. My mind maintains on reminding me, "you have got unfinished gadgets still geared up." Therefore I pick out listing topics because it makes it clean for me to get on by supporting me prioritize duties and get matters finished inside the constrained time availble.

No be counted variety variety what your motivation is in the back of list subjects, projecting responsibilities in the form of To-Do lists is an high-quality manner of undertaking all your obligations and decreasing stress.

A small exercise :

Go through your To-Do list and take a look at which pending project is making you uneasy.

What to do subsequent?

Take the list and layout a step-via-step plan for the very last touch of the most essential undertaking. Place that critical venture in your To-Do list for the very subsequent day.

Did this lessen your restlessness?

Chapter 4: What Results In A 'Flop' To-Do List?

When I say a To-Do listing allows streamline each day, weekly, month-to-month and yearly duties, I advise a 'properly-created' To-Do listing, and no longer simply any list. Many human beings try to create and use a To-Do list to kind out our troubles. We draft one hoping to hold order, and of route to be on-track and stop subjects on time. Those who create To-Do lists normally do it to outline their modern-day responsibilities and meet cut-off dates.

I receive as genuine with the ideas behind a list, at least in precept. Despite those motives, maximum human beings fail even as growing and the usage of a To-Do listing – Why?

The list we create generally receives too massive and subjective, which makes it hard to paste to. Most of time, it makes a speciality of the incorrect devices, giving them extra priority and in doing so, devaluing the simply high-quality duties.

When we create a poorly deliberate listing, we are in fact which includes to the stress on us in place of resolving it. This might be the cause maximum people discard their lists and blame loss of time – which isn't the actual purpose.

A To-Do list, if well created, can in reality assist remedy this trouble. A appropriate To-Do list is one which permits us to prioritize effectively. Unfortunately, that isn't always often what occurs because of the list no longer being created well via the purchaser, and so obligations fail to be correctly prioritized.

One purpose for why most To-Do lists don't artwork is that our grading of high significance is sincerely too huge; as a end result our list of what is pressing receives way too big and we come to be tagging the entirety as very important. Because of this our list appears to pay hobby on the wrong obligations at the incorrect times. This outcomes in strain and frustration, and we surrender, questioning the list simply isn't walking.

Another very not unusual but important reason may be procrastination. This is one element that blocks the road to fulfillment. It obstructs our way near aiming on getting topics completed expeditiously and in a properly timed fashion.

What is Procrastination?

Procrastination is our movement of delaying or suspending things in place of attempting and completing them on time. Most humans are the sufferer of procrastination in the end. Too often we decide on having amusing now and getting critical things achieved later.

There are varieties of human beings — ones who create the listing, however procrastinate on the subject of following it thru, at the equal time as the alternative form of human beings avoids growing a lsit within the first region.

Forget a well or poorly created To-Do listing; inside the first place, maximum humans procrastinate developing the listing in any respect. They offer form of excuses for now not doing it: heavy art work load, no time, don't apprehend wherein to begin from and a few can't decide whether or no longer to put in writing down on paper or use digital medium for making one.

In order to eliminate this trouble, you need to understand and address the number one motive for procrastinating.

This purpose(s) prevents you from reaching fulfillment and reaching the new heights. By identifying the actual reason on your procrastination, you can paintings at correcting this and overcoming it.

In the previous couple of years, there have been a number of research accomplished into this whole region of procrastination. Some of the commonplace reasons they located are:

- Feeling tired

- Fear of failure

- Inability to prioritize

- Distractions

- Lack of motivation

- Lack of interest

- Lack of interest.

Once you realise the cause(s), with the resource of way of developing techniques you'll be capable of combat procrastination. Once you triumph over this addiction, you'll be able to finish duties extra efficaciously.

In the following financial ruin I'll listing some of the crucial factors to be avoided even as growing a To-Do list.

Chapter 5: What To Avoid While Framing A To-Do List

Before we communicate approximately a manner to create an efficient To-Do list, we first ought to put off the behavior that spoil the writing of or the implementation of your list. Habits that we've got got have been given advanced, in all likelihood without even identifying, over time might be the reason why you are not finding fulfillment along aspect your To-Do list.

You might have noticed no matter you list the entirety (from small to huge), you are not capable of hold a right tune of obligations and not able to complete it within the given period of time. This indicates that there may be some thing that you are not doing effectively and it needs to be steady proper now.

Before we attempt to overcome wrong behavior, it's miles in reality essential to realise what to avoid even as developing a

To-Do list. If you want a viable list, you can need to observe the following:

- Avoid Itemizing Things on Any Sheet

Now I comprehend you'll say, without a doubt that's what a To-Do list is for? Prioritizing duties, simplifying existence and remembering stuff resultseasily, right? But does your listing serve this purpose? Did you honestly say "NO?" Do you realise why? It is due to the fact you create To-Do lists on random scraps of paper, receipts, payments, diary or any pocket book. And while you listing obligations on random sheets it will become tough to prioritize your gadgets. Instead, make it much less tough for your self and attempt to make list in a committed pocket book, laptop or cell utility, so that you don't need to rummage through multiple sheets to prioritize chores.

- Don't Draft a Lengthy List

A suitable list is one which is short and candy. It is critical to be specific approximately every undertaking you listing, soak up and aim to complete. But at times, we turns into overly unique and as a manner to complicate even a simple undertaking. There can be times whilst you need to provide an motive of an assignment, but you shouldn't get over excited and emerge as writing an essay. The aim want to be to create a listing that might goal essential information and might with out trouble be interpreted at a look. If the entries are too extended it might make things seem too momentous and you will likely grow to be doing no longer a few element.

- Don't Generalize Things

When I say be particular because of this you shouldn't be too desired. Create a listing to recollect stuff without problem and end it inside a stipulated time period.

Just like I stated above, write a listing that is straightforward so that you can do not forget. Draft it on this type of way that while you examine your list, you may now not have to spend more than a minute thinking once more to recall your motive inside the returned of list a particular component. The clearer you're, the more effects your thoughts will recollect it.

● Avoid Listing Everything underneath One Category

One of the most crucial errors people make, which is also truly one the various maximum critical motives inside the back of the failure of a To-Do listing, is mixing non-public, professional and every day responsibilities below the equal class. I in my opinion feel, and I'm as accountable as the subsequent individual, it's quality to create separate education for the ones three differing forms of venture. This will simplify prioritization and make it greater consequences executable.

● Avoid Listing Far-off Future Tasks (http://lifehacker.Com/)

It is outstanding to listing everything you are making plans to do, which incorporates writing destiny obligations for your To-Do list entries, but it's miles important which you don't burst off too some distance into the destiny to the issue which you switch out to be getting pressured about which undertaking to soak up first. If you don't want to reflect onconsideration on a selected undertaking for some weeks, listing it in separate class (may be some element like a 'Someday' class), and check out it even as it genuinely starts to draw near.

● Do now not Overstuff Your List - One of the most not unusual reasons why To-Do lists fails is that maximum people upload a protracted way too many devices on the same listing. Some oldsters placed such hundreds of factors on our list to try and perform internal a single day on our list that we get overloaded and try to carry out what must commonly take consistent with week to finish. Overstuffing your listing reasons big amount of hysteria, and this uneasiness consequences in low-amazing art work. It decreases your productivity and too much strain can also have an effect on each your bodily and your highbrow fitness. A To-Do list gives and takes. A To-Do list lets in us keep in mind and stop obligations on time, but most effective if drafted effectively. At the identical time, if a To-Do listing isn't created because it need to be, can result in a noticeably-forced, disturbing and threatening existence. So it's far commonly recommended to be practical at the equal time as creating your listing.

• Don't Give Yourself Too Much Time — A tendency to be lenient on ourselves about deadlines consequences inside the failure to a To-Do listing. The extra time you allot to a particular undertaking, the more the chance which you'll by no means have the capability to finish it on time. There is a procrastinator in each one of us, and the more time we offer ourselves for completing a undertaking, the masses plenty much less possibly it is that we'll nail it inside the given time slot. Therefore it is in reality important to set an genuine time period for every project at the listing. Also allocate time consistent with the individual of the art work. If a small assignment can be finished in an hour, you have to make a be aware about the proper time body.

00003.Jpg

Try and take a look at the ones factors to stabilize your listing, which in turn may additionally moreover furthermore enhance your productivity. It may be very clean to allow a To-Do list get out of hand. If you're having an trouble turning into the whole thing in every day, week or month, http://lifehacker.Com/ indicates you revamp your To-Do list to experience a greater organized life.

Re-writing a To-Do List

Redoing your To-Do list proves useful in lots of methods. The most important gain is that while you rewrite your list, with the aid of revisiting your responsibilities you could double-test for errors and timing errors. By doing this you could evaluation your dedication to every object and make certain you better optimize a while.

It could probably appearance really stupid and time-eating to re-write your whole list, however doing this you'll with any luck take away any useless duties choking your day, and get to the bottom of what truly wishes to get finished.

I recommend an clean approach to re-write a To-Do list. Check below:

● Spend 10 minutes re-writing a brand new each day To-Do listing

● Prioritize duties in keeping with their relevancy and importance

● Categorize them into pressing (to be completed nowadays), secondary (may be finished in each week) and excursion responsibilities (may be accomplished at a later date e.G. In a month)

● Take up 2-four priority duties you'll have the capability to finish thru EOD (surrender-of-the-day)

● Create a separate elegance for 'Holiday Tasks' or 'Someday Tasks' — obligations you don't seeing doing these days.

In the following financial disaster I'll let you know how a To-Do listing, if written effectively, famous the individual of its creator.

Chapter 6: How A To-Do List Describes The Story Of Your Life

Each one people has the addiction of writing notes or list devices that we desire to don't forget and whole. Some write in a systematic way, even as others surely scribble on a chunk of paper; a few humans pick retaining a separate To-Do list ebook, at the same time as others choose writing on any random scrap of paper. With the advanced generation of in recent times, a few techno junkies use To-Do listing apps to observe their important responsibilities on their favored device. In whichever organisation you compromise, your To-Do listing does greater than genuinely be aware of your duties, it well-known your character and defines your individual too!

When a person makes a listing, in reality they're writing their lifestyles tale. Your writing famous your thoughts – things you are planning for the destiny. The closing dates you write in competition to every venture describes your capability i.E. How speedy you'll be capable of do it.

Your listing depicts in conscientious element what you have got carried out, what you are planning for the future, in which you're going, which obligations you supply most priority to and what genuinely subjects to you from the day you made a decision to start writing a To-Do list.

Although a To-Do list appears at face price to be only a boring list of everyday duties, in fact it well-knownshows an character's life information. Even when you have in no manner met that individual, his or her listing might assist create an photograph of him or her. Some human beings may additionally need to even relate to a person showing the identical tendencies after studying their list. There are a few who're stimulated via analyzing any other man or woman's list and are then stimulated to create a list of their very own.

Each individual's fashion of making a listing is one-of-a-kind. Some choose extreme detailing, at the equal time as others focus on information the huge photograph. I for my part feel an excessive amount of detailing makes the list too big and complex, thereby making it difficult to complete within the selected time frame. I comprehend a friend who usually specializes in detailing, which at instances reasons hassle for her – most of time she not noted an crucial ultimate date. In case of being overly unique, our time can trickle away earlier than our listing is finished.

As I highlighted inside the preceding bankruptcy, it is right to be specific, however being over-precise can fast complicate even a sincere task. The goal need to be to create a list which could purpose important records and one that can be effortlessly interpreted at a glance.

Our To-Do listing defines who we're and what our choice is. There are a few folks that maintain writing duties with out bothering to perform them. Their listing is more like a story, shooting every second, hour and day, and lots less like a actual, duties-to-be-checked To-Do list.

After studying some lists, I found many people have incredible attitudes with regards to their To-Do listing writing conduct. I determined that even though folks that are very techno-satisfactory often despite the fact that pick out listing their responsibilities the conventional way – with pen and paper. Most of them have reasons supporting this addiction; a few say they enjoy crossing items off upon of entirety of every assignment. A few people amongst my contacts stated they sense more responsible in the direction of a listing they hand-write than one that they kind on their laptop structures, laptops of medication.

As I referred to in the sooner paragraph, I actually have moreover come across many lists in which the makers write the greater a part of their lists in code. There is a reasonably obvious reason why a few human beings use code for his or her lists. While there may be not whatever wrong in writing a listing in code, the most embarrassing 2nd comes even as the code used is really too apparent. No offence, but this normally takes place with woman listing-makers. Sorry, ladies! Some write To-Do lists to simplify their lifestyles; a few write because of the fact they revel in the process of listing-making, whilst the very last describe themselves as 'triggered' listing makers.

What sort of a list maker are you? Take the fast workout underneath to discover!

In the following chapter I'll screen how a To-Do listing allow you to stay a healthful, efficient and strong life.

A brief exercise

To find out what shape of list-maker you are, solution the questions beneath:

- Do you use code phrases to put in writing a To-Do listing?

- Pen and Paper or Digital Devices — which of these do you pick to create your To-Do listing?

- Are you a committed or a compulsive listing maker?

o Finding this is straightforward — in case you take out day out of your busy time table and create listing for day after today and repeat it each day, you are without a doubt a devoted list maker!

● Think: even as became the very last time you made a To-Do listing? This will help you make a decision whether or now not you are a dedicated list-maker or you're stimulated!

Chapter 7: A Good To-Do List Means A Healthy And Stable Life - How?

The middle concept inside the again of growing or keeping a To-Do listing is to prepare one's life and end each project on time. Whilst we're aware about it permits to growth productiveness and stay an organized existence, I'm advantageous now not plenty folks apprehend that To-Do list is also useful for your fitness.

The hyperlink among a To-Do listing and accurate health is properly-documented through way of http://wearelikeminds.Com/. It has been recommended that folks who frequently hold a To-Do listing realize that doing this is about greater than just creating a listing of things to do on a specific day and time. It is the maximum critical pressure reliever.

Many human beings assume too much paintings approach too much pressure.

They experience stress comes with overloading of obligations. But a famous blogger Scott Gould believe that strain is advanced on the identical time as we don't understand what to do i.E. Whilst we don't have anything to do. That's particularly genuine and I can vouch for that in my view!

Imagine you're in a computer magnificence, have a pc and net connection however don't recognize what to do. How will you enjoy?

Most people anticipate that it's miles having stuff we want to do, however aren't capable of obtain (for any given reason) that creates problems in existence. Writing can reduce your problems. Just as writing stabilizes your thoughts, writing about the dreadful incidents of existence will let you cast off them at the basis. This in flip also limits the effect of these episodes on our bodily health.

Writing your issues down helps you to offer you with solutions. Once you discover a way in your trouble, you'll enjoy relaxed. This will lessen your anxiety.

You can check this out for yourself. When you experience uneasy because of the pile of obligations for your inbox, write down those obligations in a list and outline priorities, and you may immediately start to revel in calmer.

We stay in a time wherein the speed at which we get hold of information is remarkable immoderate and the picks we've got were given are limitless; ultimately feeling beaten at instances is natural. Once we listing devices on paper, we find out them less difficult to recollect them and revel in greater accountable to them; this exempts us from the danger of things slipping from our minds or records overload.

Listing simplifies existence; it furthermore motivates us. As noted earlier, a To-Do list helps to make lifestyles higher organized, and assist a coordinated man or woman cease each challenge on time and recall crucial activities and dates. This shape of man or woman is preferred in both their private and professional areas. They are considered reliable for the entirety and identified at every degree. This will growth their morale and arrogance. So on this manner a To-Do listing can enhance your intellectual fitness at the side of bodily.

For a stable and healthful lifestyles, we should continuously write limited devices in our To-Do listing. In his ebook The Ultimate Guide to To-Do Lists — How to Effectively Create, Manage and Use To-Do Lists to Get Things Done, Gordon Sharp talks approximately a observe executed with the useful resource of the usage of Sheena S. Iyengar and Mark R. Lepper published in December 2000 and entitled Journal of Personality and Social Psychology. The have a observe well-knownshows that our brains can control approximately seven options earlier than we sense crushed. So therefore, we need to be very cautious even as drafting out To-Do lists. We need to take care that if we have got more than most type of devices in our listing, we'll sense hammered with fear and anxiety, and this can lessen our actual art work extremely good.

To conclude, listing-making can lessen stress, thereby benefitting our physical, intellectual and emotional health.

Are you feeling beaten? Do you've got too many duties to your listing that is hampering your mind from achieving every one? Don't worry! In the subsequent monetary destroy, I'll give an reason for the manner to prioritize duties for your To-Do listing and acquire your goals.

Chapter 8: How To Prioritize Tasks In Your To-Do List

"Which venture should I begin my day with?"

This is one of the maximum not unusual questions we asks ourselves. If you may take my recommendation, you will take within the venture which you are least searching ahead to do first. Doing such assignment prepares you for a extra powerful day and solid destiny. Want to know why?

We all have one assignment ordinary which we time period because the "worst assignment," and don't want to do it first. For the most green day, define your "worst project" a day earlier than, and list it as your first project of the following morning. This will come up with peace, due to the fact the issue you considered worst you had already ticked out out of your To-Do list.

Quick Tip for a Productive Day – "Always plan your day after today an afternoon in advance than."

Once done with the worst challenge, you'll revel in a extra acceptable time and enjoy assured and terrific in the route of the day. In his book Eat That Frog, non-public development professional Brian Tracy makes use of the vintage idea that in case you consume a frog first problem in the morning, you'll already have the worst mission over with early on and everything else will seem clean.

Never cast off a project, specifically one you dread. Remember, when you procrastinate you may need to spend your very treasured time on the equal assignment each morning. But in case you intend to finish it, you could get it executed and the pride of seeing the maximum daunting project crossed off your To-Do list is matchless.

Completing the painful project from your list shouldn't be your most effective challenge. The next venture you should aim to triumph over is to ensure you time desk chores realistically.

Most humans have To-Do lists longer than their going for walks day. It is real we have 24 hours in an afternoon, but out of this time how many hours are possible – we have to don't forget that first. A person can art work for not more than 12 hours an afternoon (even this isn't feasible every day), productively. If stretched, the artwork acquired't be our wonderful first-class. Despite know-how that we've were given a finite length of time in hand for operating, we create 14 hour-prolonged schedules and attempt to wholesome all of them right into a 9 hour-lengthy artwork-day. After incorrect scheduling, we surprise why we aren't able to finish duties as in keeping with the list after which we are saying lack of time is the precept hassle while the problem is with our list-writing technique.

The exquisite manner to time desk duties is to match your To-Do list together together with it slow desk each day. If you apprehend a assignment will take 3 hours, write precisely that during your listing. If you end it in advance than time, nicely and top, but don't count on subjects earlier than definitely doing it. Similarly, block at the least one hour from your time table for "Emergency Tasks" and closing 15 mins of your strolling day to be aware about in that you stand and consequently time desk the subsequent working day. Try this and word the trade on your recurring!

The biggest problem with folks who experience overburdened and aggravated is over-scheduling or list unrealistically. I'll supply a sensible instance which all working humans is probably in a function to relate to – your supervisor may additionally additionally assign you a assignment at the ultimate minute and ask you to supply it on Tuesday (assuming in recent times is Monday). What people typically do in this situation – to pride their supervisor they're pronouncing "effective, outstanding" with out consulting their time table, it is pre-deliberate for the following day. The outcomes of this willpower come while work brought is of inferior nice or if a challenge task changed into compromised to complete the final minute mission.

While it is good to oblige managers, it's far in addition crucial to stability subjects. At this level the pleasant factor you can do is are searching for advice out of your agenda and solution some questions – will this task healthy inside the one hour emergency time slot that I've steady for this form of emergency? If you get a "no," offer an motive of for your manager, in case you take in this venture, you'll need to compromise on the opportunity one from the list – is that ok? If it isn't, tell him you could deliver the today's venture on Wednesday. But be very clean at the outset.

One element that working professionals constantly whinge about is that maximum of their time is going into weekly reputation calls with customers or inner conferences. In that case you need to try to speak for your immediate boss and attempt to lessen the amount of conferences you need to attend, especially in case you are running on tight closing dates. If the assembly can be finished thru a cellphone call or thru video conferencing, cancel the face-to-face meeting and make the selection as an alternative. Try to recall methods to reduce conferences to hobby greater in your real responsibilities.

Highlights of this Chapter

● Block at least one hour to absorb emergency or on-the-spot obligations

● Keep at least 15 minutes apart on the give up of your strolling day to plan the next day

● Be practical at the same time as planning your time table.

I desire those elements will assist you to prioritize your duties. In the next financial ruin, I'll offer an purpose in the back of the capabilities of a realistic and executable To-Do list.

Chapter 9: Features Of A truthful And Workable To-Do list

Most folks have our very own fashion of creating To-Do lists; a few may want to possibly determine on making plans their next day earlier, on the identical time as some may moreover furthermore start their day jotting what to do for the relaxation of the day within the morning – each person has their personal fashion of writing To-Do lists. But some techniques of listing responsibilities are commonly higher than others; now not each style is fruitful.

There are amazing traits of a To-Do listing, which if taken into consideration at the same time as drafting your plan, will assist you acquire or regain productiveness and decrease strain.

● Advanced education – One of the maximum practical matters a To-Do List creator need to do is to take a few hours out to pen down all the critical obligations which you need to complete in a particular time span. One must commit a short time for making plans and streamlining duties. Obviously, it is predicated upon on you the way a whole lot time you want to dedicate for growing a To-Do listing. Some professionals plan consistent with month, at the identical time as others plan quarterly. On the other hand there are a few individuals who plan their upcoming day the midnight earlier than. Whatever fashion you've got, enhance planning is an important detail of a a fulfillment To-Do listing.

● Dissect Tasks – Once you decide at the duties, have a look at them and word what the demanding situations are, what more you'll require for completing the obligations listed. For this, ask your self some questions – are they a one-shot undertaking, more complicated or more than one-movement obligations? If you enjoy it's miles complex, then your subsequent plan-of-movement need to be to interrupt down these huge duties in severa smaller responsibilities. See, your hassle is solved!

● Detailing – Although I said in financial disaster 5 to avoid being too specific, I didn't advise to say depart a project incomplete. In order to finish a project effectively it's miles simply essential to feature certain information which can be critical. Adding statistics makes undertaking accomplishment easy. For instance:

Wrong style: Visit medical doctor at eleven:00 a.M.

Right fashion: Visit the pores and pores and skin expert at 11:00 a.M. And speak your allergy in element, ask him to endorse cleaning cleaning soap and weight-reduction plan to keep away from this problem in destiny.

This makes challenge accomplishment quick and clean.

• Prioritization — As I've already stated this issue in Chapter 8, you want to attempt to prioritize duties for a greater powerful day and strong destiny. When I say prioritization that doesn't advise just numbering every undertaking as 1, 2, 3 or A, B, C. If you've got got were given an extended To-Do listing, it makes sense in case you categorize each venture into 'vital', 'much less crucial' or can be completed 'in the long run'. (refer Chapter 1 — All approximately To-Do List for clarification)

• Option of digital or physical — This is based totally upon on private desire. Some human beings are extra snug using pen and paper, at the same time as others decide upon going digital. Many people say writing the use of pen and paper gives them a experience of relaxation and makes execution clean and brief. On the opposite, others discover it higher listing obligations of their Smartphones or laptops, the use of a devoted app.

● Best in form approach – Every man or woman is particular and so is their listing-making style. One need to no longer get over excited with the aid of diverse humans's recommendations on the subject of list-making. It is first rate to determine out what works fine for you rather than following the crowd. It frequently takes place that a pores and pores and skin cream that quality suits you, may not wholesome your pal. Similarly, a listing-writing fashion that fits your pal may not fit you. If I provide you with my example, I choose not more than 3 items in my every day listing. With greater responsibilities, I discover my pressure degrees increase. However, for some humans from the identical career having an extended listing is pressure-decreasing because of the reality that ensures a few improvement is made on the whole lot every day.

• Customized Solutions – Sometimes a clean To-Do list isn't beneficial for a few human beings. Although prioritizing is essential, some people want to take more steps to simplify their complex existence. This is normally the scenario with great personalities. For instance, an military chief or President has a much complex and large mission listing even as in evaluation to a mean man or woman. The feature which they're in technique they'll need a software or system that does some of their duties like sending reminders and alerts and automatic scheduling. If your life has come to be very stressful, maintain in mind a tailored solution.

In order to find out custom answers for every problem it's far in reality critical to determine what's maximum critical to you, and then doing it to acquire fulfillment and peace in life. And the way to determine this?

It is likely one of the most tough sports. The exquisite manner to determine which undertaking want to be on the top of your priority listing is ask your self a smooth query – which undertaking, if I don't cease these days, goes to disrupt my sleep and damage my highbrow and physical health? The first issue that comes on your mind need to be numbered 1 in your To-Do list.

• Seamless Changeover – What is our normal day like? Some obligations to complete, a few commitments to satisfy and a few paintings to assign. In brief, our commonplace days are a aggregate of factors we do for ourselves and for others (buddies, circle of relatives, circle of relatives or colleagues).

We switch from one function to each one of a kind for the duration of the day. We wake up as a woman, prepare breakfast as a spouse, feed as a mom, artwork as a professional in an workplace, behavior meetings like a supervisor, meet friends for dinner and visit dad and mom like an fantastic daughter. We usually execute many obligations during a day.

What keys out the To-Do list of an powerful person is their recognition that our lives must tour seamlessly at some point of borders, in location of focusing and coping with in fact one region or characteristic. The key to a green and happy life is blending every professional and personal paintings (notwithstanding the reality that in precise education) for your To-Do listing for existence to feature with out interruption.

Short Exercise:

Create a To-Do list the use of the tendencies indexed in this financial ruin. At the stop of your venture listing, test whether or no longer or not you've got got finished (or maybe progressed a touch) what you have got were given deliberate for the day/week/month.

In the very last but no longer least critical chapter, I'll listing the names of top apps to help you draft and manage your To-Do listing.

Chapter 10: Top 10 Applications To Create And Manage Your To-Do List

I had generally been an propose of pen-and-paper. But I changed into finding myself sinking increasingly more every day, with a pile of hard work and no time to finish it. I had sticky notes tucked proper here, there and everywhere. My To-Do list end up on the verge of turning into unmanageable. Suddenly, I began to enjoy crushed. Does that sound like your tale?

One Sunday even as I become sitting at the window thinking about what have turn out to be happening to me, and questioning if something grow to be incorrect with my fashion of execution or have become it the list itself failing me. After an hour of Q&A with myself, I determined: the hassle have come to be now not with my listing-writing style, the actual trouble changed into with the traditional method I modified into following.

From that day I changed my listing-making supply, and switched to cellular application. Now I'm succesful to plan and check my precedence at the identical time as at the bus or at a espresso preserve. Today, I revel in I'm more powerful and masses much less confused and beaten.

If, like me, you make a decision to use technology to put in writing and manage your To-Do listing, the alternatives are infinite. Each software has its private execs and cons. All of them artwork, and they all have troubles, so it in massive part is predicated upon in your preference and which app you're most comfortable with.

In this financial catastrophe, we'll assessment pinnacle To-Do list apps. Check out my listing below:

1. Wunderlist (https://www.Wunderlist.Com/) – Popular as one of the fantastic loose apps, Wunderlist have a graceful interface and lots of first rate capabilities. It lets in automated syncing and preference to personalize the format. Users can create subtasks and connect and detach sticky notes. You can share and collaborate with buddies and circle of relatives, and use a nifty "interest center" to manipulate the popularity of responsibilities, obligations and lists. The landscape layout of Wunderlist gives a huge view of upcoming projects and duties. Wunderlist's real-time sync right now maintains all your lists updated no matter in which you're.

2. Evernote (https://evernote.Com/) – Write, collect, find out and gift, Evernote does it concerned in you. It is likely one of the most well-known word-taking apps. Although the clean Evernote is

unfastened, in case you end up an addict and want more capabilities, you could buy the pinnacle price model. With an fantastic synchronization characteristic, you could sync Evernote with numerous computers, pills and Smartphones.

Although it isn't always exactly a To-Do listing maker, you can make it act like one via using activating its checkbox characteristic. You can percent notes thru electronic mail, outcomes insert images and audio clips and prepare objects through manner of date, tags and location.

You can create and upload folders indoors folders. Additionally, you could get right of get entry to to this app online and offline. This is excellent specially whilst you are visiting and function troubles with connecting to the net, you may nevertheless make adjustments on your To-Do listing and all of your adjustments can be synchronized as fast as your connection is another time.

3. Todoist (http://todoist.Com/) –

Calling itself one of the global's maximum effective To-Do list apps, Todoist moreover lets in you to artwork with and with out internet connection. Thanks to its HTML5 foundation, Todoist is specifically fast. It lets in you to percentage responsibilities with every person – pals, circle of relatives, and co-employees- and collaborate on shared plans and desires.

Some of the exciting competencies of Todoist encompass actual-time information synchronization, you may get notifications, visualize your productiveness, more than one priorities, set reminders and plenty of extra. It offers a neat, clean and streamlined appearance this is appealing to those seeking out a streamlined life.

4. Remember the Milk (http://www.Rememberthemilk.Com/) – A free software application, Remember the Milk is greater than most effective a To-Do list-maker. This is a software program software that may be used to kickstart with most effective a easy list-retaining method, but once you get greater snug with the interface, you will want to explore more competencies.

The excellent function of this app is you could prepare your responsibilities into tabs and acquire automatic reminders about a particular challenge. You may additionally even sync this software with Google Calendar. Like Evernote and Todoist, you may moreover manipulate your obligations offline.

Remember the Milk is a whole project-manager device. You can percentage duties for walking with organization buddies and might get right of entry to this gadget out of your Smartphone as properly.

5. Doomi (http://doominow.Com/) –

What is quality about this Abode AIR app is that you may download it to your laptop. You can down load the app, enter duties and move them off and note what you've got already finished. The app sends properly timed reminders to do a selected undertaking. It offers each on-line and offline synchronization alternative as well.

6. Google Tasks (https://www.Gmail.Com/mail/help/obliga tions/) –Almost anyone has a Google account nowadays, so it's herbal to show to Google Tasks for developing a simple To-Do list. You can add, edit, pass off and delete responsibilities as you need to. It offers us the sensation of a traditional pen-and-paper listing-making style. It is unfastened to use.

7.   Errands   To-Do   List
(https://itunes.Apple.Com/in/app/errands
-to-do-list/id318095638?Mt=8) –

This app gives a calendar-based in reality manner to control your responsibilities plus symptoms to ensure you don't forget to finish the venture on time. You can also upload a new item in your listing, set up folders, installation precedence degrees, due-date and due-time. For a top level view of your responsibilities, you may moreover have a take a look at monthly calendars that show duties due on remarkable dates and times.

Created with a mixture of clean and advanced abilties, Errands To-Do List is a mission manager with specific features: checklists, folders, signals, computerized badge updating, mail duties, calendar view, scheduling & repeating, a couple of view modes and masses extra.

8. Any.Do (http://www.Any.Do/) –

If you are planning to apply this app, congratulations you'll be capable of keep loads of it gradual! Any.Do can expect mission-related textual content at the same time as you type. You can drag and drop, swipe to mark responsibilities as whole, and shake your device to easy completed projects. It allows clean sharing of notes and duties.

9. Bla-Bla List (http://www.Blablalist.Com/) –

Bla-Bla is completely unfastened. It offers clean-to-use-and-share To-Do lists that use Macromedia Flash. It allows sharing lists with others regardless of the fact that they don't have an account. Bla-Bla permits you to position up your lists with RSS just so others get straight away updates and also can see how your duties are progressing. Additionally, it permits you to proportion your lists privately with anyone and paintings on them collectively. You also can e-mail yourself a duplicate of your list.

10.   Orchestrate (http://onlineapplications.Net/) −

One of the blessings of this app is that except letting you arrange your To-Do list, it allows you create many lists, every with its very personal call. You can create a listing to hold the agendas of upcoming meetings in this app.

Other self-explanatory specialised listing-making apps:

● Remindus (To-Do Task Reminder) − https://www.Remindus.In/

● Baby Pack & Go (Family Packing app) - http://www.Babypackandgo.Com/

● Grocery List Maker (an app for grocery shopping   for)   - http://www.Grocerylistmaker.Com/

- The Universal Packing List - http://upl.Codeq.Data/

I'm not saying you have to use technology on your To-Do list. Of course that's your non-public choice and in case you are most cushty with pen-and-paper, don't be dominated through awesome humans's selections. Figure out what's high-quality for you.

Chapter 11: The Psychology Behind Time Management

There are 3 essential factors to time control. Those are: recognition, corporation, and dedication. Being aware of not great the significance of time manipulate, however the factors that inspire your distraction method you could address and exchange the ones problems.

Awareness

Awareness manner it's time to apprehend the significance of it gradual and rate variety it as a give up end result. No greater the use of excuses for those initiatives you did not want or can not see the purpose for, no greater preserving off the truth that you could rather be everywhere else. It is time to encompass your focus of all the elements involved, well known your choice to no longer do the project on hand, and then recognize the importance of doing it except.

It is likewise critical to be aware of the ones times for your day in which there are a couple of desires and expectations, in evaluation to times that are a good deal a great deal much less scheduled and consequently available to devote to a totally unique venture. Do not expect that allows you to do the whole thing right now. While there are quality 24 hours in a day — and face it, you want to sleep sometime — it's far although viable to set apart less costly time blocks for the severa subjects on your life that want performed. By organizing your time desk wisely, time manipulate is already enhancing.

Organization

Being organized lets in for higher time control and further fulfillment in accomplishing desires. Seeing the capability for issues to get up or information that a few topics can't be multi-tasked technique you can arrange the day as a end result.

Organizing a workspace is likewise important to higher time control. Time spent deciding on an area for the whole lot and continuing to hold items in their assigned places way considerably a first-rate deal much less time spent searching out a specific document or device this is typically wanted proper that second.

Some people declare their creativity is stifled through employer and cleanliness. A naked workspace does not stifle your creativity, but, it surely permits it to flourish in an organized and minimum placing. This absolutely encourages your creativity with out giving it parameters at its jumping off factor. Keep that during mind the following time your boss glares at you accusingly over your cluttered workspace.

Commitment

The willpower is the manner to advantage the ones goals. Not being distracted or lured into procrastination is the cease end result of willpower to the try at hand.

Commitment way your strength of mind gets you through the ones urges to test your e-mail or take one more stroll to the harm room. It allows you attention on checking responsibilities off your to-do listing that have been completed in a mature and fantastic manner.

Of the 3 elements, commitment is the vicinity you've got were given most possibly failed within the past. Therefore, the attempt will focus right right here the maximum on the manner to find out prolonged-term achievement and the functionality to combine your to-do list mastery in techniques that increase productivity in all areas of your existence.

Chapter 12: Define Goals and Motivation

It isn't always feasible to trade and manipulate time higher without private wants to carry out the alternate. If your conduct annoy your boss, your partner, or your buddies – that isn't always sufficient.

What do you preference to get out of better organization: extra money, more reputation on your profession, or among buddies or in truth, better extremely good of life?

Any of the above goals, on the facet of countless others, can be sufficient to electricity someone to make high-quality changes to their productiveness and employer. However, that is the requirement: desires for you and you on my own.

SMART goals

Now that you have located your why for attempting the mastery of to-do lists, and with those to-do lists your existence as an entire, you can begin to attempt for SMART desires. Yes, this means desires which might be smart to purpose for, however it moreover has a totally large that means to characteristic to every goal you place.

These goals are:

•Specific – The Five W's come into play proper right here. Make splendid for the purpose you may answer Who, What, When, Where, and Why.

•Measurable – Set a way ahead of time to decide in case you are meeting your desires, a particular "yardstick" if you could, to degree if you have carried out what you hoped to do.

•Attainable – With your schedule, and all of the distinct factors of your existence, are you capable of see your self mission this? If no longer, it is time to re-draft.

•Relevant – Goals you area are in your advantage. Therefore, do now not searching out to win an award in a place you are not inquisitive about simply to affect someone. Do subjects you will be glad with and set desires as a result.

•Timely - A time body for very last touch and the capability to mention, "Yes, I really done that aim," are important here.

Another manner to outline desires, brought inside the ebook, Made to Stick through Chip Heath & Dan Heath, is SUCCES, moreover known as sticky dreams. These desires are:

•Simple – The easy concept is without difficulty shared.

•Unexpected – Out of the everyday or no longer "the norm."

•Concrete – Ideas with numerous statistics usually stick the remarkable. Stories surpassed via generations are nicely examples.

•Credible – You should be given as proper with it took place to a person else.

•Emotional Stories – You empathize with the people within the story.

Now you are asking, how does this set of criteria look at to your to-do list goals? It is as easy as this: those form of dreams draw close your interest. Obviously, emailing the group does not capture your hobby and hobby like growing a today's piece of paintings or an ad advertising and marketing marketing campaign for a cause you take delivery of as true with in. So, create your desires with the ones requirements in thoughts, however no longer a have to on each purpose. This offers a degree of newness to your questioning and permit you to grow to be greater nicely rounded if not anything else.

It is crucial to break a big reason into smaller goals. This is easier to degree and time table so you can watch your self art work inside the direction of that big goal. Having the huge reason and now not the use of a measurable steps in the direction of attainment makes distraction and procrastination that lots easier.

Having smaller steps toward the very last ultimate date makes it less complicated to take breaks to recharge your batteries or to get small rewards en path to the huge payoff.

What's retaining you again

It's time to address the devices that intervene together with your diploma of manufacturing. First, make a list of factors most usually get inside the manner on the same time as you are trying to move gadgets off your to-do list. If you're certainly starting to area into effect to-do lists, make a listing of things that distract you or more days each week on a regular basis.

Distractions can absorb as an lousy lot as two hours of your day. This approach a massive dent within the wellknown time set apart to be powerful.

At hours in step with day, seven days regular with week and fifty weeks in keeping with three hundred and sixty five days, you spend a median of 57,512 hours distracted (based on a mean U.S. Lifespan of seventy nine years). Obviously, with some effort, at the least a part of that factor may be positioned to lots better use.

One of the most critical elements that impedes, distracts, and stops a fulfillment time control nowadays is social media.

Having immediately get admission to to unique individuals of the group via numerous sorts of communique may be beneficial. The capability to analyze at the run is manifestly lots higher than being caught in a library for hours or days just to find out the concept you're getting to know falls flat. However, the disadvantage of those obvious advantages is the get proper of entry to to topics you may be living with out.

There is not any reason to check in with pals or antique excessive college buddies on a each day basis on Facebook. There is not any absolute need to recognize straight away through notification or electronic mail which you acquired an invitation to a endeavor on any amount of social media structures.

Finally, to be honest, now not everyone desires to have the capacity to test their e-mail every quick time. Yes, a few critical business enterprise offers are executed with the useful resource of sending documents via e-mail. It is right that negotiations can be finished through electronic mail as properly. However, for nearly all parents, checking e-mail every minutes or with each harmonious ding is in fact detracting from the momentum we need to have in the direction of the finishing touch of the venture earlier than us or the concept this is slowly getting into being at some stage in a brainstorming consultation.

Natural Tendencies vs. "The Way Everyone Does It"

Have you observed you accomplish subjects more effects within the morning or the night time? Set apart time for the ones responsibilities while you're maximum probably to acquire achievement in their of completion. Not honestly each person is made for a 9 to 5 workday or maybe success ultimately of daylight hours. If you typically will be inclined to find out greater creativity or more ambition within the afternoon or night time, do not try to pressure your self to artwork tougher inside the morning. Things will no longer schooling consultation on your favour.

Instead, make certain to prepare it sluggish desk on this kind of manner that you'll reap achievement. If you start off slow inside the morning however have a propensity to hit the ground taking walks after lunch, make your to-do list with a whole lot less hard obligations for morning hours and the bulk of your jobs set for afternoon completion.

Finding non-public strengths is essential for masses reasons in lifestyles. Knowing what you are maximum captivated with and especially proficient in paves the manner to fulfillment as a terrific deal as being prepared and efficient. Think outside the field to determine the first-class approaches on the way to technique a mission or the regions of the challenge you realize you do extremely good. The subsequent step is ensuring to continuously positioned greater weight on the belongings you are right at in a scenario but allow extra time for the areas that you apprehend as out of doors your talent place.

Chapter 13: Organization/Preparation

To-Do Lists – Organize them!

One huge trouble with a to-do list is that you brainstorm all the belongings you need to do, and the listing will become prolonged and intimidating. With the form of lengthy list, it is simple to surrender earlier than you even begin. This manifestly falls a ways brief of the productiveness degree you have been hoping to obtain.

Introduce a 2d step. Once brainstorming is complete, create 4 (or more) separate lists that during shape your life and streamline the items into orderly businesses.

For instance:

•Household obligations

•Errands to Run

•Work-Related Tasks

- Calls to Make

- Upcoming Events to Prepare For

Then set a time frame for working on each list, like an hour for own family duties, and focus on only that listing. Make advantageous every listing is tackled at some stage in peak hours for you in terms of ambition and energy. Don't go away the paintings duties for while you're already worn-out and dreaming of your head hitting the pillow. Mastering your to-do list is a stepping-stone to productiveness in all elements of your existence. Be high-quality to be honest and targeted if you need to succeed.

Color Code and Digitize

When it involves to-do lists, there may be no such thing as having them too precise. Color-coding is a superb way to show the priority degree of each challenge.

One approach of color-coding is the website website traffic mild machine. Red is for need to be performed, amber is for buying near reduce-off date, and green is for the duties which you understand are on the horizon, but nowadays might not bypass down in flames if you push off this venture for tomorrow or maybe day after today.

If you do now not experience the colour-coding desire, move for labeling responsibilities with precedence letters. The letter A, as an example, can be obligations that HAVE to be carried out these days. Letters B – E have to have various tiers of importance, with say D and E every being tiers that can be postponed as important.

Having multiple to-do lists is not a manner to acquire achievement. If you discover yourself creating a listing, misplacing it, making every exceptional and then even a third on paper, your cell smartphone and your pc — it's time to find out one approach and live with it. In that vein, locating a virtual app that crosses out of your smartphone in your laptop and again is a first-rate answer.

Leading Apps to Get You On Your To-Do list way

When turning to generation for help growing to-do lists, there are infinite apps available that would truely make it easy and inexperienced.

Below are numerous examples, every focused on specific factors and a possibility on your ideal assistant in to-do listing mastery:

Evernote: A exquisite software to be had on Android telephones. This app allows for notes in paragraph or check mark layout. It moreover integrates photos. A primary account is free, and with a username and password, a to-do list you have got were given created in your cellphone and saved can be accessed from a computer at the same time as your mobile phone battery has died or you have got 3 things to feature and no concept in that you located your phone.

Todoist: Available on any platform. This app is similar to an e-mail inbox, with due dates, mission enterprise employer and the capacity to share with others who may be worried.

Wunderlist: Available for iPhone, Android, Windows, and Kindle. This app is a extra aesthetic alternative that still permits you to categorize and sub-categorize to your coronary coronary heart's content material cloth material.

One Note Mobile: Available for Android, Mac, and Windows. This app is a wonderful one for the colour categorizing minded. This app has the capability to grow to be a easy check list or it could be paragraph form. For this app, each list may be a unique colour so you realise without studying which obligations you may be taking on.

Remember the Milk: Available for Android, Mac, and Windows, syncs with Google and Calendars. This app is high-quality for simplicity in inclusive of the duties and it already divides into artwork, non-public, check, or maybe immoderate priority designations.

Google Tasks: Web, Windows, and Android. This obviously works with Google services. It connects along with your Google account and works with email and the calendar to make your lifestyles streamlined.

Clear: iPhone. This app is aesthetically charming, with pinches, swipes and drags included into venture creation. It works nicely with the iOS, and it recognizes the show show width of the iPhone.

Orchestra: iPhone. This app allows challenge task to everybody with an email deal with and contact range, no matter the truth that they don't have the equal app downloaded. If a group all has the app downloaded, the task assignments can be seen with the resource of all and discussions can be had through the Orchestra app.

There are infinite brilliant apps available, with both unfastened and paid variations, in each the Google Play hold and the App Store for Apple customers. Obviously, the unfastened variations have fewer alternatives. However, this could help for those who do not want greater confusion in the advent of a list. The paid versions can be the way to transport if your list is prolonged and complicated, with more than one sub-training and important differences. Only you could make those alternatives.

De-Stress

When it includes growing productivity and enterprise, it is critical to now not increase the stress you placed on your self to acquire. Instead, take a look at the adjustments as possibility for increase. Recognize your shortcomings exist. The terrible conduct may be triumph over, but it's going to take time.

Focus on the positives and the little successes. Reward your self for those and forget about the issues, apart from to element them in for destiny responsibilities. This approach a lot less stress on your psyche and some other decorate, but slight, in your productiveness tiers. Having a mantra or a remarkable quote to reputation on each time matters get overwhelming or you have were given had been given the preference to throw up your hands is a amazing way to keep pressure degrees at a minimum.

Some useful expenses** I in reality have determined are:

•If it is purported to take vicinity, it's going to. If it isn't always, it may not. You can not trade it. Therefore, no want to fear. Problem solved.

•God didn't do it all in at some point. What makes me anticipate I can?

•The feeling of strain is crippling, just like the whole lot in existence it to is relative. Stressed? Change the point of notion from poor to excessive exceptional. Easier said than executed because negatives are usually much less complex to look. Positives want aware idea and typically a few form of movement to be visible.

•When pressured, take a time off to loosen up your muscular tissues and lure up.

•Stressed spelled backwards is desserts. Coincidence? I suppose not!

•The time to relax is whilst you do not have time for it.

•Everything relies upon on you and inside the identical time you can not benefit the very last intention by using your self.

•The mark of a a fulfillment man is one that has spent a whole day at the financial institution of a river with out feeling responsible approximately it.

•Being glad may not endorse that the whole thing is right. It manner that you've decided to look past the imperfections.

•Appreciate the demanding situations you're going through right now, for just like the butterfly you shall fast emerge from it higher, more potent, and further lovely.

•Pain is truly short, but dropping because of the truth you finish will grasp-out you all the time.

•What will wreck you down isn't your burden but your way in carrying the weight.

•When some component goes wrong for your lifestyles, absolutely yell, "Plot twist!" and drift on.

•Giving up is simple, at the same time as your dreams seem some distance away.

And life is whole of barriers, you face them regular.

But, no matter what the task,

Some faith will get you thru it.

So by no means prevent believing.

Remember, you CAN do it.

**All attributed to unknown or anonymous.

Chapter 14: Planning Your Day

Is the primary task of the day making your to-do listing? If so, you're already within the again of.

Taking 15 mins from the day before to make the list and having it in the front of you while you are making it to the place of job the next day, approach more productiveness both on the prevent of in some unspecified time in the future and the beginning of the following.

Mornings may be gradual to begin, so already having a to-do listing receives the engine revving that plenty faster.

Estimating how lengthy will it take / delegation

An vital trouble to think about at the same time as considering how hundreds time to set aside for every undertaking is The Principle of Least Effort. This principle, brought with the aid of the usage of

Vilfredo Pareto (1848-1923), is likewise referred to as the 80-20 Rule.

The eighty-20 Rule states that 80-percentage of output is produced through 20-percentage of input, or further, 80-percentage of consequences are produced thru 20-percentage of reasons. In one of a kind phrases,

This can are to be had in reachable while making plans out the time and effort required for obligations with the aid of manner of recognizing the 20-percentage of gear as a way to be used most at some level within the project and having them near hand. Convexly, 80-percentage of our time is spent on results that are not almost as extraordinary ultimately.

The rule can also assist through manner of figuring out the peak instances of the day in that you accomplish the most (your 20-percent most effective duration) and aiming to get 80-percentage of your success from those hours of the day.

Finally, this is available in to be had even as delegation is essential to get greater paintings completed quicker. If you recognize the those who are handiest for unique obligations, delegating 20-percentage to that person or group approach 80-percent extra effectiveness due to the fact they're the most green man or woman for the venture.

Stay on track

Set take a look at-ins for improvement and divide the bigger duties into small desires which are extra without hassle measured and deemed finished. When a massive project is assigned at paintings as an instance, divide the project and deliver your self cut-off dates for studies, interviews, or reality-locating, element A of the assignment entire, and so on...

It is also an incredible idea to set an earlier reduce-off date for yourself than the final reduce-off date. This lets in time for those final info that continuously crop up and need to be filled into the very last hours.

Having a mindset on the direction you are headed is especially beneficial with reference to being more inexperienced. That method having goals set for some weeks or a month within the destiny, six months in the destiny and then a year inside the future and so forth. This offers a very concrete way to make sure you discover achievement along with your to-do lists and more difficult to quantify goals. These lists can span the term until the following reason.

When setting the desires, recollect the time every step in a to-do listing can also require. If the to-do listing is walking in the course of a goal that may be a yr within the future, some steps may additionally take a day or every week, even as others can also take months. Put these in an less expensive order and supply them the right time strains.

Technology may be a benefit in terms of keeping yourself targeted and heading within the proper course with time traces. There are programs to be had, like Leech Block, StayFocused from Google, or an app known as Focusbar from Apple, that lessen off get proper of access to to social media and super websites that inspire distraction all through positive durations of the day or hours every week.

Being honest with yourself and taking the preventative measures for those behavior you've got placed hard to interrupt is a huge step within the course of integrating the to-do list and being a hit with it. Face it, individuals who apprehend how to hold from distraction do not commonly pick out up the books on Time Management. With the writer being a hardcore procrastinator, you are in right organization.

The Not-To-Do List

We're speakme about to-do list mastery. While you are operating on this, it is a high-quality concept to create a no longer-to-do list. This listing covers all the horrible behavior you've got that dispose of from the time you spend being green. This is the listing of factors that get in the way at the identical time as you are trying to maintain close a to-do listing.

The first steps to growing a no longer-do listing are just like the strategies to create your to-do listing.

•It must be done in a quiet vicinity.

•Look at past sports activities and ones for the following couple of weeks. Consider obligations that do not meet your cutting-edge interest description and/or lifestyles dreams

•Write down the things you want to feature to a now not-to-do list.

•One object that need to be on the list is, "Say sure to the whole lot." This has an inclination to seem so you should make others glad. Remember you need to be happy moreover.

A final element is you want to percentage the now not-to-do listing. If it's far specially work-focused, it desires to be shared together together with your colleagues, secretary and your manager. The people around you want to apprehend that you are trying to be efficient and deciding on up duties that do not suit your interest description or aren't for your high-quality hobby do now not do you any precise.

A now not-to-do list, like a to-do listing, should be updated and revised frequently. Keeping your self in line involves each carrying out the matters for your to-do listing and information your doing subjects that cast off from that. This is wherein attention is a huge problem.

Commitment is available in with the ordinary revising.

Here are a few various things which are exceptional additions on your not-to-do listing.

•Don't consciousness on or (worry approximately) future sports or subjects which you cannot control.

•Don't placed large strive proper right into a project or venture which you recognize in advance of time won't be a huge have an impact on on on anyone's life or profession enhancement.

•Don't surround yourself with humans you cannot accept as true with or be satisfied round.

•Don't attempt to exchange others.

•Don't overlook to delegate whilst possible.

Chapter 15: Reward Yourself

Having a number of smaller goals set en path to a huge cause is a way of praise in itself. However, being capable of set specific small rewards for responsibilities executed manner you're much more likely to locate the ambition to paintings on greater of a to-do listing.

Seeing the reality that you completed - thirds of your to-do list in a day, as an example, gives a sense of self-self notion and lets in you to look what strategies motive achievement. With those smooth in your thoughts, it's miles possible to move in advance and be aware that diploma of fulfillment in the future.

It is essential to be taking walks closer to three element at the same time as conducting desires. The pride of a mission properly-performed, at the identical time as a few component, is not enough to maintain you assembly immoderate standards you've got got set. Instead, offer your self set breaks that let you relax and interest your energies in exclusive pointers each day. Also, set larger rewards for as quickly as a massive intention has been executed. Trips or awesome acceptable matters that are not a part of every day existence are a extremely good way to reward yourself on the equal time as you gain a aim.

Breaks are NOT Rewards

Here is a extraordinary time to take a look at that forcing your self to paintings from begin to finish without breaks isn't always the maximum inexperienced time scheduling. Giving yourself a ruin from your to-do list and attention at the obligations accessible is not some element to bear in thoughts a praise.

Breaks have to be scheduled in at instances you understand you begin to lose momentum. Or, if you aren't high quality whilst in case you want to be, provide your self an concept of what you'll do at the same time as that takes place. Say, a 15-minute damage for a espresso or a quick stroll across the block at the same time as you're doing household responsibilities. Another concept at the same time as on foot errands is a couple of minutes to visit an area that relaxes you, like a garden or park, to recharge the batteries once they begin to run low.

This is any other reason scheduling your day realistically is crucial. It lets in for the ones breaks and unexpected troubles that would – and commonly do – pop up.

Rewards Can Be Anything Important to You

For some humans, rewards need to be physical and visible to the rest of the area.

To others, a easy moment to shut one's eyes and bask in success is enough.

This entire procedure is ready increasing your productivity. Tailor any rewards machine to helping you benefit dreams and encouraging you to do better and art work extra tough. If you are a bodily praise-type, get an extra caffeine jolt or go to an area you like for lunch, despite the fact that it is a chunk out of the way. Buy a brand new e book or blouse or watch, something will make you glad and be a seen reminder that you did in fact nicely at the side of your goals. This can be a massive assist if the next day's listing does no longer bypass as without difficulty.

Incentives are reinforcement, overindulgence can be counter-green. As prolonged as you notice the difference some of the , you could take your to-do list and productiveness to new heights.

Chapter 16: Tricks for the Best To-Do Lists

Obviously, on the identical time as this e-book is assisting you form an knowledgeable records for developing a to-do listing and all of the common experience in the back of the hows and why of the artwork, it hasn't to date confident your mastery of a to-do list.

Get The Best Start

Below are numerous tips if you want to give you a leap-start inside the route of that reason of mastery.

•Use a template – There are infinite internet web sites available that could provide templates on your to-do lists. Easily accessed via way of a easy Google or Bing are trying to find, web web sites like Getorganizedwizard.Com, offer templates which is probably unfastened and interactive. These templates will assist you to with saving cash, promoting devices, studying cloth, and your weekly schedule, amongst distinct focuses.

•Write down all of the responsibilities you'll come across and spend time on that day – This gives you a higher concept of a manner to allocate time at the same time as although turning into to your lunch ruin and getting a bath.

•Start with some clean stuff – Particularly at the start, beginning the to-do listing with three to 5 easy responsibilities that can be crossed off fast and provide you with a cushion of fulfillment is right. This will increase self notion and consequently productiveness. Leave the extra hard responsibilities at the way to require longer periods, like an hour, for the middle of the list.

•For Every Hard Task, Do a Few Easy Ones – Here is also a manner to present your self a self belief improve. If one in each of your duties takes an hour, ensure to time desk three smooth five to 15-minute duties for at once afterwards. This gives your hobby a breather at the same time as you still tick off gadgets that want finished. You are a lot much less probably to get discouraged and beg off on closing obligations whilst you preserve moving but get a hazard to take a step returned at the identical time.*

•Make Your To-Do List at the End of the Previous Day – As stated in advance than in this e-book, it's far best to have a to-do listing already created earlier than the day starts offevolved. That manner, you can ease into the day with the easy obligations in desire to stressing your self out looking for to do not forget all the stuff that HAS to be completed.

*These hints come from Travis Steffen's article posted at Forbes.Com.

Tips To Help Even To-Do List Pros

Other crucial thoughts, those from LifeHack are:

•Deal With it When You Find It – One massive hassle with procrastination is encountering a mission or idea and thinking you may get again to it. If you're checking your electronic mail or discussing a few difficulty with someone, do not located it off. The idea wants to be scheduled, assigned or filed at the time it plant life up. That saves time later for other obligations to be addressed. It additionally decreases the risk of it being out of vicinity or forgotten and thereby ignored out on.

•Weekly Reviews – Schedule a time, the identical time every week, to have a take a look at what you've got finished, what has gotten through manner of way of you and what has yet to be completed. This is a exceptional time to evaluate a success techniques and failed attempts and be aware about improvement for your attempts to increase productivity.

•Structured Procrastination — You're thinking, WHAT?! Well, for those who are proper at self-deception, you can use your very private tendency to location subjects off to increase productivity. If you are having hassle collectively in conjunction with your to-do lists, shape them so the responsibilities at the top appear critical to finish and vital. In the middle ought to be greater critical duties that look an lousy lot less onerous and extra thrilling. These responsibilities will ACTUALLY be individuals who need finished more brief. Congratulations, you've got have been given truly tricked yourself into procrastinating at the responsibilities that can be put off and finishing the ones which can be more vital.

•ToDon't List – For all those belongings you discover yourself doing that detract out of your productiveness. Write it down and preserve the listing near, so that you undergo in mind now not to do those subjects at the same time as you are within the quarter and getting topics completed.

•Music – Music can be substantially powerful in decreasing you off from individuals who through hazard (or deliberately) intervene along with your attempts at productivity. Use headphones. Even if you are a person who receives distracted through song, use the headphones except. No one else has to realise you sincerely can listen them over the "music" for your head.

•50-30-20 – This is the branch of time to spend on responsibilities for lengthy-term, middle-term (years or much less) and straight away (subsequent 90 days), respectively. This is every day, thoughts you. Each day, 1/2 it slow must be spent at the prolonged-term, or large image. One-1/3 of a while need to be on the center-term part of your life and the 20-percentage is on the immediately future.

•Do Your Worst – Rid your self of expectations for perfection. Simply undertaking the venture is going an extended manner. It is not important to gain it within the maximum form viable .

Chapter 17: Where Do We Go From Here?

So, right right here we are. We talked about the manner to set goals, the first rate instances to put in writing down a to-do listing, and the strategies to prepare them, wherein to jot down down them, the way to shade code them, or even the manner to decide out the satisfactory chance of success (The eighty-20 Rule).

Simple. If you've got were given got by no means written a to-do list in advance than on your lifestyles, begin small. Sit down and write 3 to five stuff you plan to get performed day after today.

Organize them from most vital to the "ah, that-can-wait-if-it-has-to" mission.

Make nice the list is someplace effortlessly accessible. Have an idea of even as every task can be finished inside the direction of your inexperienced hours.

Look again on the chapters in this ebook and hold in thoughts when you have covered all the vital bases. For instance, did you:

•Define the Goals you preference to obtain?

•Organize your List?

•Plan the Order to Best in shape your fashion?

•Set rewards to your private mind for high-quality elements alongside the manner?

•Find at least guidelines to help you be triumphant?

If you revel in your to-do list is enough to get your obligations completed, it's time to get some rest. Get to the list early and observe in which it takes you.

Once you have had been given gotten to the forestall of the day, evaluate your fulfillment. Consider any unforeseen issues you had or large interferences with your techniques for this primary day. Write the next day's to-do listing with all of this in mind, in addition to the subjects that went absolutely well.

Repetition and versatility emerge as crucial for the following few weeks until you discover the nice rhythms and behavior to preserve excessive levels of success. Do the topics that bypass well over and over again. For the duties that needed more time or have been not scheduled at the first-rate time of the day, consider the ones instructions on the equal time as strolling on a brand new to-do list.

Being a Happy Person with a To-Do List

Being a achievement, growing productivity or perhaps de-stressing have been touched on in the course of this the way to on getting to know the to-do list. One final thing, be glad with lifestyles.

Be bendy for the ones times while subjects genuinely aren't going to go proper. Then, after they do, be sure your rewards degree as plenty as the successes you are experiencing.

Understand the weather and severa different factors are going to weigh in. Even your tendency to procrastinate goes to pop up on occasion, except you are a real Zen draw close of the to-do listing. Even a draw near has an off day, in any place.

In the give up, the excellent trouble is to find your groove with to-do lists, as with each different assignment in lifestyles, and revel in the natural moments while they come. Don't permit lifestyles pass you via manner of because of the reality you are targeted on fulfillment, productiveness and the to-do listing.

Chapter 18: 7 Mistakes that Makes a To-Do List Highly Unproductive

We all make errors now and again on the things that we do. Especially if they may be something that we do for best a brief at the same time as.

When we make use of the to-do list first time, we'd do a little issue wrong that makes it now not capable of offer its advantages. These wrong strategies are clearly the topics that we want to apprehend so we are able to repair them. In the long term, we will enhance our to-do list implementation manner so it is able to later provide us the favored blessings. When we recollect it, how are we able to do the proper development if we don't understand things that we should enhance? It is the simple principle of the improvement method for all of the additives of our life.

Yet, it's far regularly now not smooth to recognize the wrong topics that we have were given got achieved associated with our to-do list implementation. The loss of records of these mistakes makes them completed for quite a while and they become a dependancy for us. When they have end up behavior, it may be greater difficult to restore them. We might in all likelihood assume it's miles part of the to-do listing implementation that makes it really works for us.

For instance, we may additionally moreover regularly create to-do list project elements which might be too substantial. Those mission elements may also furthermore consist subjects which incorporates completing a mission for our company or improving the sales of a product. These forms of factors may want to make us stressed approximately what are the subjects that we have to do to finish them. They confuse us in region of giving us readability concerning the of entirety of the subjects that we need to do. As a result, the to-do listing that is composed of things like those brings little improvement to the productiveness of our paintings.

When it involves acknowledging those mistakes, we can also no longer capable of do it. It is because of the reality the mistake is something that we've got already finished for a long term regarding our to-do listing usage. It have end up a trouble as we maintain doing something that gives us little or maybe contrary consequences of the meant advantages. We might also honestly create the to-do list due to the fact we have got have been given have been given used to it. We don't recollect the productivity benefits that we assume from the device.

Therefore, it is able to be important to perceive what are the mistakes that can be related to the to-do listing approach. It is absolutely so we recognise whether or now not the mistakes are some issue that we do in our implementation as nicely. We may additionally have greater knowledge on their implication and connect them even as we understand why they damage our to-do listing utilization. After all, it appears there may be little need utilising a to-do list if we make the mistakes in its implementation. Those errors that makes us can not enjoy the advantages that we want.

To assist you with figuring out the mistakes, here are 7 predominant mistakes for the implementation of a to-do list. They might be the subjects which you although presently accomplish that it is higher to repair your to-do listing additives speedy. Especially at the same time as you think they could bring awful influences in your try to prepare your works optimally.

Mistake #1: You Have Too Much to Do

When growing a to-do list, it could be tempting to take the very excellent path and just listing all of our works. However, it might not be the high-quality approach to put in force. It can result in growing a to-do list it really is precis and sincerely has too many things taking region in it. The responsibilities listing of this nature will no longer deliver the intended readability that we are able to get from a to-do list.

There can be massive topics that we want to complete in our days. For example, we may also want to finish solving and cleansing our residence or revise our art work until our manager authorized it. When we see those forms of matters listed, but, it is probably demotivating due to the reality it's far too full-size to comply with. We can also don't have any concept what we ought to do to complete the fixing and cleaning or complete the revision till legal. They are too fuzzy and can be drilled down better approximately the sports that we need to do to complete them.

The mistake of making too complicated factors make us want to anticipate difficult just so they'll be appeared as completed. This can possibly waste our time and decrease our productivity as we strive to determine out our to-do listing which means. The technique should make us also doing things that are not intended for the terrific consequences of our art work approach. This all because we try to outline how terrific we can finish the duties in our to-do list. We may additionally need to have an excessive amount of to do as a end result and that isn't appropriate for our artwork's effectiveness and overall performance.

Besides having too much to do because of the obligations' ambiguity, the mistake also can be associated with the obligations amount. Simply through having too many responsibilities indexed can confuse us regarding what we need to do in a day. The implementation of this to-do listing must make us bewildered of which is probably the responsibilities that genuinely want to be finished in recent times. Our time is confined so we might become doing the duties which is probably not too crucial in assessment.

It may be clean to simply list all the matters that we want to finish on our to-do list. However, this error within the method can confuse ourselves while we try to do them. It also can even decrease our productiveness as we don't comprehend what are the proper sports activities in our strolling hours.

Mistake #2: You Have to Do Things That Are Unclear

Besides too many stuff to do, we can also be burdened via the unconcreted trait from the responsibilities that we list.

It is usually less complex to get the grip of a few aspect tangible in place of intangible and the quantitative in preference to the qualitative. When we've got responsibilities which may be intangible and qualitatively measured, it may make us surprise whether or no longer or no longer they've already been finished. The results is we also can prolong the time that is used to finish the project. It is due to the reality we do not recognize what's the defined stop line for it. Furthermore, we may lose motivation because of the fact we don't recognize how can we artwork for something that has no concrete desires.

The examples are on the identical time as we listing a few aspect like enhance our business enterprise or enhance the appearance of our lawn. Because the elements do not have easy goals in them, we might also moreover spend an excessive amount of time walking in them. We may additionally additionally even no longer paintings on them the least bit due to the fact we don't recognize what we can do to carry out them.

The duties which might be too hard to define may be an critical issue of the paintings that is useless and inefficient. When we don't recognize the things we desire from a manner, then we received't recognize how the technique should be long-established. This will lead to an unproductive effort. We attempt to create some thing that we do not apprehend the best necessities are. This is why a enterprise form of the outcomes that we want from our artwork is crucial. We will apprehend what form of hard work ought to we deliver and what type of try must we located into the gadget.

Moreover, while you want to diploma the effects to your expectation, you want to have some thing tangible you can evaluate. This is related to the subsequent to-do lists moreover as it may use the scale end result for its machine device. The missing quantifiable variables out of your task's factors will make it lots greater difficult to try this measurement and evaluation approach. As a stop end result, you could manner too overestimate or underestimate the art work which you do. This will affect the to-do listing that you try and create for the following time.

Mistake #three: You Have Too Easy Tasks

When you want to be powerful, then you in fact can not without a doubt do your paintings with a so-so mentality. You need to push yourself so you can artwork optimally close to your most functionality.

If you use a to-do listing, then the way you list your responsibilities is critical to determine your productiveness. Sometimes, we need to take it easy through listing the responsibilities that may be finished with out problem in a quick time. This isn't consistent with the actual benefits that we want to get from the device.

We may get a few pride due to the fact we're in a function to finish all the obligations that we've were given already targeted so early. However, if we want to chase long-time period fulfillment, then this will bring about a far longer time for us to prevail.

Having too clean obligations listed is not best due to the fact it is able to emerge as a strong reason as a way to procrastinate. When we don't recognize what else to do, this is the time which we're susceptible to the urge of procrastination. When this is the case, due to this our to-do list absolutely turns into the device that offers us validation to procrastinate. We could possibly think, anyways, the to-do list has been already finished. We ought to use the remaining time to loosen up for the relaxation of the day. The to-do listing that we create for productiveness has simply grow to be the primary motive to do the opportunity. This is surely no longer an fantastic addiction to put into effect in our to-do listing usage.

Listing too easy duties may moreover even now not push us to develop for my part and professionally. One of the maximum crucial lessons that we will acquire may be had via the research that we were given. The maximum valuable opinions normally come from the difficult stressful conditions that we are going thru. When we handiest aim for the smooth ones, this is while our self-improvement development can also furthermore stifle. This trouble might also have an impact on the future of our productivity. That is because of the truth the extra you apprehend about the way you ought to work, the greater green you are in getting outcomes. As your increase is halted with the aid of the easy obligations' testimonies, the risk to be extra powerful in destiny works isn't precise.

It is simple to fall into the lure of making subjects too fun through placing no longer-so-tough objectives that we should accomplish. However, the fantastically green people would probable pick the hard ones in choice to the smooth ones.

The criteria are the responsibilities are regular with their preferred consequences. Moreover, they want to be no longer too difficult that it may become a few other mistake in formulating the to-do listing. The mistake of creating it too hard is what we are able to talk approximately subsequent.

Mistake #four: You Have Tasks that Are Unrealistic

It is all proper if we need to venture ourselves to finish all the obligations which we regard as maximum fruitful. This can supply the enormous advantageous self-boom that we want from the experience of doing them. However, there may be a case furthermore of listing too many duties to do in our to-do list. This mistake may even prevent the productivity benefits that we want to get from the device. Unrealistically difficult responsibilities can grow to be one of the most critical reasons for our low motivation to do them.

After all, an remarkable to-do list have to make us inspired to complete the responsibilities which are in it. Not the opportunity.

When we formulate our to-do list, the overall aim is to complete all of the obligations which might be listed in a day. This is because of the truth each day is generally the cycle of a to-do list method. If we listing many obligations which usually take time to complete, then in preference to powerful, it is able to make us lazy. It is due to the fact we may think there can be no manner we are capable of do they all in an afternoon. When we already have a concept like that, it may make us even slower to do every of our works. That is due to the reality we've already out of place motivation to complete all the obligations that our to-do listing says we must do.

To make it clearer of the effect of this error, allow's say that we do a to-do listing every day. In it, we listing that we need to do a 1/2-day meeting, give up 2 evaluations, and make a presentation. If we delve into the ones obligations, then we can also furthermore realise that it's far nearly no longer viable to complete all of them. The meeting takes 1/2 of-day, possibly more if it's miles run past due, and the document or the presentation want to take an afternoon. They may also take even more if we need to provide the quality results for them.

The insufficient hours must make us lose motivation to finish the to-do list. This is due to the truth we comprehend that we truely cannot whole them. Even if we rush ourselves to finish all of them, then it maximum probably will now not be specific for the effects. The consequences are lousy because of the fact we can not do our notable for the information in every of them. It may additionally additionally even result in seriously lousy outcomes which can preclude ourselves.

As a result of this error, the excessive productiveness that we need whilst we listing those responsibilities will not be had. It may additionally furthermore additionally be tough for us to carry out just part of the to-do list. The to-do list that we've got already formulated can also end up redundant as we don't do the obligations which might be indexed.

Mistake #five: You Have No Clear Deadline for the Tasks

This mistake must in particular be had on the identical time as we don't have a easy time-body at the same time as all of the obligations must be completed. When we don't recognize the meant deadlines of these obligations, we can also commonly will be predisposed to have a decrease motivation to do them. This is because we might imagine we are able to do them every time while we want. This also can moreover result in decrease electricity of mind to complete our works, better procrastination, and, subsequently, lower productivity.

To illustrate this, allow's don't forget you're given a challenge to investigate some data. However, you don't have any deadline from your manager whilst does he/she assume that task to be completed. What will you do? Unless you assign a self-imposed closing date, it most probably consequences in you don't attempt to complete it fast. Because you don't apprehend whilst you need to give up the venture, you may put it aside to complete the opportunity obligations. You might also moreover even remove it when you have the free time to your walking hours to complete the evaluation. You provide a low prioritization for the venture. As a cease result, it's going to have a tendency to be finished in a miles later time.

The importance of the cut-off date is also being stated in the forestall result of researches. A research article done through Dan Ariely from Massachusetts Institute of Technology and Klaus Wertenbroch from INSEAD do this. It indicates that ultimate dates can assist lessen the chance which you procrastinate. It is legitimate in both cases even as they're self-imposed or while they're imposed by means of using method of different human beings.

This seems a logical element as closing dates, in particular the tight ones, make us selecting up the art work tempo. We can't give up them any time we want because of this wondering. This has an inclination to boom our productiveness in doing our works.

Deadlines can also want to make us greater prompted to do duties and their absence will make us more susceptible to abandon obligations. Therefore, it may disadvantage us at the same time as we don't supply self-imposed closing dates for every undertaking we've got were given in our to-do list. Not having last dates can also make us take time an excessive amount of in finishing responsibilities. This can result in us no longer completing the responsibilities we need to do at a few diploma in the implementation period of our to-do list.

Mistake #6: You Have a List that Goes Nowhere

Every one oldsters has lengthy-term results that they want to acquire after they do a little detail. For instance, if we paintings as an worker in our enterprise employer, then the lengthy-time period quit end result is probably vending to senior positions. If we volunteer socially, the a protracted way future very last consequences that we purpose is probably a big social effect that may have an impact on human beings. All of the works that we presently do can effect the possibility of getting the high-quality lengthy-time period results. The effect can be both notable or horrific.

The short-time period consequences can be more apparent and can be right away visible due to the fact the very last results that we get from our works. However, the prolonged-time period subjects want to just accept the eye as nicely if we need to understand them. If we want to gain massive achievement, then logically what we do each day ought to additionally make us progress to that focus on.

This is wherein the mistake may be had on the to-do list that we formulate as nicely. We don't have the give up recreation in mind even as we list the duties that we have to do. That can bring about us lots harder in conducting the long-time period consequences that we want.

If you want to attain a big success, then the obligations which you do ought to assist you in getting there step-with the resource of-step. This can't be helped via our to-do listing if we virtually bear in mind the fast-time period outcomes. The topics that we artwork on pass nowhere in phrases of the general path that they lead us to. A part of that is being supported through the to-do list that we make use of to prepare our works.

By enforcing this mistake, that also approach you aren't getting excessive productiveness from your works. That is because of the reality some of them might be no longer the right sports to get the outcomes that undergo in thoughts. One of the important elements of productiveness is the that means of the works which you do. The because of this need to be fairly relevant for you because of the fact that makes them the property you rightly recognition on. When you have a tendency to do works which don't have an effect on you certainly lengthy-time period, this means that you have wasted opportunities. These are the opportunities that can be spent to do one-of-a-kind extra crucial topics. Making the mistake of listing duties that do not in shape at the facet of your chosen lengthy-time period effects can harm this issue of productivity.

If you want your to-do list to carry achievement, you need to think of the success definition at the same time as you list duties. You ought to formulate it so the contents are exceedingly applicable to that definition.

Mistake #7: You Have Difficult Access to the List

To help you grow to be productive thru your to-do list, you shouldn't go away that list difficult to get admission to. This mistake may want to make you genuinely confuse yourself with the property you want to do in step with your plan. There are instances even as you neglect what you've got got formulated at some point of your day. Not having the to-do list nearby to remind you can affect the productivity benefits that you can get from it.

After all, one of the listing's predominant capabilities given is to remind you the subjects that you need to perform, proper? Having tough get admission to to the list in a few unspecified time inside the future of the day will forget about that feature from the tool. You may additionally run your day as though there can be no to-do listing to manual you.

The main reason for this error is honestly due to the reality you placed it in in that you can't certainly pick out out and word it. For instance, you could in reality positioned it in a paper you left or in a look at your pc can not get admission to. Worse still, you may just expect of these responsibilities in your head with out placing them somewhere you can see. That can be the mistake that makes you forget about with out hassle the responsibilities and nullify the productiveness increase from your to-do listing. And it's miles in a position to show up because of the fact you truly don't consider what's the plan you have got made in your running hours.

The mistake of no longer making your to-do list available additionally can be associated with the assignment points you have were given. Sometimes, the assignment nature is definitely some thing vital which you need to be reminded of. For example, it is probably a meeting with a person important outdoor of the strolling hours. It also can be a touch essential detail that you want to paintings in your record however it can be effects forgotten. When you're making this error, it could make you overlook those things you remembered whilst you formulate your to-do list. Those essential subjects which you have cited to remind your self is probably the key to build up the first-rate effects. You can't maintain in mind them due to the truth you truly haven't were given the easy get proper of access to to appearance your to-do listing.

****
****

And due to this, we want to be careful the ones mistakes at the same time as we want to create a to-do listing that works for us. Simply don't do topics proper within the crucial factors of our to-do listing can decrease the advantages we have been given from it. It can also even make us much less effective whilst we use our to-do listing.

Now, after we have recognized the errors, now can be the time we understand the trends that make the proper to-do list. This is vital so we apprehend the matters that we should motive for at the same time as we want to enforce a to-do listing. We will communicate deeply about the ones tendencies within the following a part of the e-book.

Chapter 19: 7 Characteristics of an Excellent To-Do List

When making a decision to apply the to-do listing tool, you need to want its top of the road advantages for productiveness and achievement, proper? Well, searching for to formulate it based totally on a few developments must assist you drastically to get those benefits.

These traits of an terrific to-do listing are given to reply each of the mistakes inside the previous financial wreck. Think of them as antidotes so you can create an wonderful to-do list that is unfastened from the ones errors. This to-do listing need to help you in guiding your works so you can advantage the effects which you want.

To optimize the working hours which you have, you need to take into account the proper sort of obligations which you need to do. You additionally ought to suppose what is the right time that you could allocate to every of them. The right shape of duties technique you listed the responsibilities which is probably meaningful for you. They additionally can be the effective & inexperienced techniques to get you to the right outstanding of results.

On the other hand, the exceptional time have to be the shortest time feasible on the way to produce your quality works. When considering the proper traits, there ought to be interest about the to-do list that would list the right duties. We have to additionally consider the device of obligations grouping which can help excessive productivity in the course of our days.

An wonderful to-do listing will guide you to make the maximum of a while. It is just so you will be glad with the results that you have produced. Simply list all of the topics which you have internal of your head received't paintings in growing a to-do listing that works. It is better which you endure in thoughts a few relevant subjects related to your productiveness at the same time as listing responsibilities. They can be your artwork self-discipline, the lengthy-time period effects that you desire, or the tangible consequences that you get. Making a to-do list that could stability all the ones factors want to be your priority whilst you select out to make use of the device.

Thinking approximately the traits that might clear up to-do listing errors and help in giving its utmost advantages may be difficult. Thus, to make it less complicated for you, you could see underneath the dispositions which need to do surely that for you. They are precise, measurable, bold, potential, time-sure, fulfillment-orientated, and available. You can name them EMAATSA in acronym so that you may moreover have an less tough time remembering them. These topics ought to help you create the to-do listing which offers you the maximum blessings in productiveness and success success.

The following additives of this financial ruin will provide an explanation for every of them in a bit. From the motive, you have were given a higher data in their software within the to-do listing gadget.

Exact

Utilizing the to-do listing tool need to make it an lousy lot clearer for you approximately the responsibilities that you want to do. Therefore, it's going to first-rate if the phrases there are sincere however thorough enough. They will make you understand precisely what you want to do. Being genuine in formulating the to-do listing is a trait that is preferred to create a to-do listing that works.

This is the feature you can use to answer the error of having too much to do for your to-do list. Exact is prepared preciseness. It is the manner you want to formulate the obligations listed in order that they will be easy and however entire. Applying the ideal characteristic to your to-do list ought to make your responsibilities more prepared. The function should provide you with a sturdy expertise of what you have to do in a miles tons less complex manner.

Being comprehensive on some component doesn't advise it should be complex and having too much content material cloth. This is the component which you want to cause to your to-do list system way. A to-do listing with too much going round should make you bet what you need to do so you can complete it. It will not be suitable for the most dependable productiveness which you aim from the to-do list implementation.

Making your to-do listing unique in proper here approach the contents within the list are easy to recognize. Ask your self those questions. Will the duties listed be easy to understand with the resource of the use of various people who seem to take a look at the listing? Will they be capable of realise what they ought to do if they are being guided by using the to-do list? Being capable of answer them honestly searching at your to-do listing have to signify that the listing already has the proper characteristic.

When having the choice to create a to-do listing that works, it is able to be easy to fall into the entice of complicating subjects. You may also moreover list all of the things which you want to be finished with lengthy purpose of each to lead them to clearer. However, that form of listing may additionally need to make it fuzzy as an opportunity for you to finish all the factors in it. The importance of creating a to-do listing which is sharp and immediately to the difficulty should take shipping of its due. This is so you can accomplish your to-do listing while no longer having to suppose yet again what you want to do. It ought to empower the productiveness advantage as you don't waste any time considering what you should do from your list. Instead, you can at once go to execute them inside the extraordinary way you may.

Measurable

Being tangible and quantifiable is a exceptional difficulty to be aware of for all the objectives that we create. This function need to make it easy to assess our development on and whether or not we've were given got hit the objectives or now not. This is a few factor that we want additionally for the responsibilities that we have were given in our to-do list. Being measurable like this is an issue that ought to be the crucial trait of our listing. Having a measurable feature have to assist us significantly in being objective related to what we execute from our to-do listing.

Measurable manner it is easy what we need to gain this the duties in our to-do listing may be considered as accomplished. The topics that may handiest be measured subjectively need to be saved away. It is because it will depend on our interpretation of whether or not or now not we have were given completed the duties or not. We may additionally additionally pick out the clean manner thru thinking about them completed even as we've got were given worked on them for an insufficient time. On the alternative, we may think our works now not finished despite the fact that we've labored on them for a long time. This may be the case if we will be inclined to look for every detail even those which aren't too critical. Those kinds of subjectivity should be avoided if we imbue the measurable hassle strongly to our to-do listing. The feature will make us capable of go through our responsibilities with out being too caught to considered one of them. The cause for being stuck can be that we don't recognise whether or not the subjects that we've got completed are already enough. This is the problem that we want to prevent by way of being measurable in our to-do list.

The clear indicator of whether our obligations are achieved or not must assist to reinforce our productiveness. Our purpose, however the whole lot, want to be that we finished all the responsibilities inside the to-do listing that we have formulated. Doing so from an first rate to-do listing have to signify that we were pretty efficient inside the day. Being measurable on our factors permits us to without problems switch among responsibilities after each of them is completed.

When we need to assess and top notch-song our art work method based totally totally on our list, having it measurable must moreover guarantee objectivity. We will recognize the price of the of entirety and can mirror to make higher planning for our next to-do lists. This can advantage us in grade by grade along with extra productiveness blessings from the subsequent upgraded to-do lists. It want to ensure that we optimize our to-do list implementation step-thru-step.

Optimally consisting of the measurable element must imply we apprehend what varieties of numbers that should gather to our obligations. This manner you can benefit your self with the know-how of the numbers that ought to accept consistent with every venture diploma. Having that information will offer you with the capability to provide intention numbers in your responsibilities which may be realistically completed.

Ambitious

When you make use of the to-do listing tool, that must suggest you need to be more powerful in your works. After all, you list your obligations due to the fact you need they all to be completed interior a certain period. Moreover, they ought to be the sports activities sports you do so you can get you the effects you preference. By together with the ambitious function on your to-do list, you may intention for the most maximum suitable result that you can get.

This feature is essential in case you want to gather the maximum and gain the very notable productiveness advantages from your to-do list. Every day we have were given 24 hours to do our works and virtually every person has had been given the same window of time. It is as an awful lot as us to optimize it to get the excellent results for our life. By being ambitious with our to-do list, we are capable of make sure that we make use of each 2nd to some difficulty enormously powerful. Being formidable method that we don't spare any attempt to finish the obligations that could supply us the favored outcomes. When we want to accumulate our results as rapid as viable, being ambitious with our to-do listing is a ought to element.

After all, one intention of the use of the to-do listing is to installation works so you can accomplish many things, proper? That is one of the productiveness benefits that you need to get from the device. Being bold want to assist you get that advantage through using manner of creating you lots more ruthless with the time which you have. No to a touch quantity of procrastination possibilities can be made to be had to us. This is due to the fact we attempt to perform maximum duties that we've registered to our to-do listing. An bold to-do list can encourage us to perform that a splendid deal more from the obligations that are indexed in there.

Being bold ought to additionally assist you in getting the first rate effects out of your artwork as rapid as you may. As a cease end result, it can moreover create a whole lot higher progress for the fulfillment which you want to attain. After all, the first-rate consequences and success can best be gotten by using the buildup of our attempt. Implement the ambitious feature in our to-do list and dedicate ourselves to get the obligations finished. When you try this, you've got with a purpose to attention on the wanted attempt each day with a better and faster way. That is because of the reality you have got were given the goal to complete the responsibilities out of your to-do list. All of the obligations from an ambitious to-do listing can offer you with lots motivation to get the responsibilities carried out sincerely.

Achievable

Despite being bold with the duties indexed, we ought to additionally don't forget the problem of hours that we have have been given. Listing ambitious duties at the same time as remembering the time wished to complete them is crucial to get the most out of your list. Keeping your elements viable is essential so that you don't revel in too overwhelmed through the scale of duties you need to carry out.

Having the duties which may be finished internal our listing's time body will naturally manual the selection to complete them. After all, we comprehend from the system that all of them may be finished realistically. Believing the final touch of all our obligations is smart can keep us targeted to do every of them quicker and better. A to-do list that is formidable but unrealistic can without issues make us lose the inducement to complete all of our works. We may go thru our days and we understand that we do no longer have sufficient time to do it. This is the precept effect of making this to-do list mistake, this is listing unrealistic obligations, that we should keep away from. Making your to-do list practicable need to additionally stimulate you to think about the handiest works that you need to do. You don't have a good buy vicinity for your to-do list to join up all of the works that you may take into account. Naturally, you have to best pick out out the things which are maximum important to be worked on. Creating an capability to-do list will make you plenty more selective in selecting the right sports on your days. Your productiveness have to be correctly directed via list and doing super the matters that you seriously ought to do. The time whilst you formulate your to-do listing play a crucial feature in making your artwork device more effective and green. That to-do listing then will become the guidance which you need to make your works having the proper form of productivity.

The time period "potential" for the characteristic of your to-do list furthermore pertains to the assets which you have currently. The most productivity need to be received thru having a to-do listing that may optimize assets to excellent aid your artwork device. Focus on the feasible duties based truely at the to be had assets whilst you formulate the to-do listing. Doing that must assist you to listing the obligations that you may end without considering the property you don't have. That unneeded idea can also lower your productiveness whilst you do the art work. You will lose the incentive to finish the duties which can be hard to do with the resources that you presently have.

Time-Bound

When you have got some objectives that you want to collect, it is critical that you set a time-sure feature for them. This is the thing with a view to ensure that you may be an entire lot more area in optimizing some time. Having this function for your to-do list should offer you with greater motivation to artwork. In turn, it will advantage you with more productiveness to complete the works that you have indexed in it.

The time-positive characteristic want to be cited concerning the period which you should spend and allocate continually for all of your responsibilities. As described earlier inside the e book, loss of time constraint may be a detail that lowers our productiveness for a task. The cause is we have a propensity to provide low prioritization to the ones responsibilities because of the reality we feel we are able to give up them whenever. This is genuine in particular in case you haven't grown a sturdy strength of will to complete your works. Adding the time-sure function for your to-do list must nullify the problem. It also can deliver the guidance that you want associated with the prioritization of your responsibilities.

Having a time-certain function should additionally deliver us extra hobby concerning the assessment and great-tuning technique of our art work method. One of the maximum referred signs in identifying our productiveness is the time that we need to complete our art work. Having the time-nice function can be the way to look whether or no longer or now not we are effective or not in executing our to-do listing. In turn, we might beautify the settings of the time limit for the duties in our subsequent to-do lists. The time restriction shouldn't be too tight and permit us to do our extraordinary works. We also can beautify our art work approach so we will gain the idealistic dreams which we've got set. Because of this, the time-certain characteristic can come to be the catalyst of the productivity advantage we get from our to-do list. This is particularly associated with the time wanted to finish our works.

A to-do list with time-high quality traits should offer you with an urgency sense as long as you're devoted to complete it. When you execute your to-do listing, think about the time constraint as some thing that you ought to meet. As a result of this, you ought to be able to enjoy the effects longer. Finishing your responsibilities faster may moreover come up with the observe-up opportunities that you can't get if you end your obligations slowly.

Success-Oriented

Surely, you need the outcomes of your art work to give you a few thing vast. Regarding this, there may be nothing higher than those in order to carry you a bargain in the route of the existence achievement you want. Success is a few aspect which you have a strong preference to achieve and that goal can be helped thru your to-do listing. This can be the case so long as you look at the achievement-oriented characteristic during your to-do list approach manner.

A achievement-oriented feature need to make you list the tasks which can progress you to the fulfillment which you want. This manner that the consequences of your paintings must be straight away or circuitously correlated with the terms of your fulfillment. Your paintings outcomes ought to have a wonderful deal less which means to you if they can not make a contribution to the long-term success you preference, proper? By having fulfillment-orientated tendencies, you may popularity on the obligations that can be felt more good sized when you have finished them.

Building the to-do lists which may be fulfillment-oriented need that will help you to be greater constant in operating toward your achievement. Success, anyways, is something that should be constantly worked for. So, the to-do listing need to come up with a massive benefit related to the success which you want to benefit. Always looking at your desired achievement will make all of your duties to examine the equal pattern and characteristic the equal cause. This form of to-do list will help you to seriously offer more hobby and hold you moving in advance towards your goals. That must help you in retaining on course with the short-term and prolonged-time period consequences which you intend to carry out.

By thinking about fulfillment even as formulating your challenge points, you could postpone obligations that aren't suitable in terms in their effects. They even possibly want to now not be worked at all due to the fact they may be not consistent with your desired prolonged-term outcomes. The success-oriented characteristic will help you considerably almost about listing the crucial responsibilities that you want to do. Your to-do listing permit you to to be extra selective on the subjects that you have to and shouldn't do.

Being success-orientated for your to-do listing approach you want to balance a number of the short-time period and the prolonged-time period consequences. This interest should make you extra productive associated with the massive accomplishments that you want in lifestyles. You need to have this characteristic in particular in case you want a to-do listing at the way to assist you to to accumulate achievement in existence.

Accessible

One crucial function of a to-do list is to remind you approximately the vital topics that you need to artwork on. This is so you can optimize your day and make yourself as an alternative green. In this example, the way you remember the crucial duties that you need to do may want to have an effect to your productivity. If you've got a exceptional memory of them, then you definitely received't do the works which don't convey lots effect to you. You gained't spend time considering what you want to do subsequent after your current mission is finished. For your to-do listing to do that feature optimally, it should have the to be had function. Thus, you can effortlessly check it whilst you want some guidance of the works you want to do.

Think of the to-do listing as a cheat sheet that you may test if you overlook about what you need to do. Having the chance to have a examine it again and again must moreover make the obligations plan stick themselves to your thoughts. As a stop give up result, the chance that you forget them even even as you don't have a take a look at your listing may be decreased. That could make you be greater easily go through each of the responsibilities that you have.

It can be understandably difficult to don't forget all the duties listed as you undergo the day. Especially if the duties encompass small subjects that want to be remembered to artwork on. When you're in your walking hours, your attention shift from one project or occasion to some other. That will make you masses greater susceptible to forget about about topics that are not associated with the current mission that you do. When a to-do listing will become available to you, it is able to manual you for the shift amongst obligations. You need to have a company information of what you have to do in the course of as you're guided constantly thru your list.

When you try to examine the available function in your to-do listing, because of this you need to have the list nearby. This is so you can see it as you need it. The to-do listing may also have critical statistics that you expect crucial in the course of the time whilst you need to do your obligations. They may be important while you attempt to finish the duties to get the excellent results. By having your list without issues accessible, that want to enhance the danger of it makes you keep in mind the ones small but essential matters. That may additionally have an impact to your productivity genuinely as you don't pass over any single component that permits you produce the great consequences. You may also moreover even produce the results faster as you recognize the specific things that you want to do for the assignment.

So, you have got were given recognized deeper about the EMAATSA traits that could come up with the maximum appropriate to-do list advantages. You also can have the overall photo in thoughts of the to-do listing you can create the subsequent time you formulate it. Try to include those developments so that you can save you the errors that have been described within the previous chapter.

In the subsequent chapters of the ebook, we are going to dig into the three techniques for every of the tendencies. Each approach may be performed to make the EMAATSA tendencies stronger on your to-do list.

In short, the techniques to reinforce every of the traits to your to-do listing may be visible in the following table.

Characteristics

Approaches

Exact

- Limit the dimensions

- Limit the subjects

- Limit the sentences

Measurable

- Search for easy applicable facts

- Benchmark the numbers

- Tie them to moves if desired

Ambitious

- Stretch your capability

- Remember the achievement arrival

- Compare the most a achievement ones

Achievable

- Look on the available time

- Think about the contemporary-day assets

- Consider the best techniques

  Time-Bound

 - Set the remaining date

- Allocate specific time inside the agenda

- See the prolonged-term

  Success-Oriented

 - Have your grand intention in mind

- Prioritize the maximum vital ones

- Reflect on the development

  Accessible

 - Write it someplace

- Make it smooth to maintain close to

- Place reminders

The 3 strategies for one function have to offer you with sensible ideas approximately what to do while you put into effect the function. You can study their explanation inside the following chapters. Hopefully, they are able to make a super excellent difference to the manner you formulate and use the to-do listing.

So, with out similarly ado, permit's explore each of them so we are able to apprehend every of the approaches a chunk higher.

Chapter 20: Limit the Scale

If you want to place into impact the precise characteristic, one issue with the intention to can help you is restricting your project points' scale. This method your to-do listing need to consist of factors that aren't too precis. They can also be effortlessly translated to the sports which you want to do.

When you do the scaling to your duties, you want to additionally ensure that the obligations aren't too small. Too small responsibilities suggest you want to listing a variety of them truely to finish an ordinary paintings. The scale problem attention is crucial while you attempt to listing the duties which have a extraordinary scope in them. It is so they may be a reliable manual for you as you undergo your day.

This method is strongly associated with the mission breakdown system that you need to do at the same time as you formulate your to-do listing. After all, any huge works which you have have in an effort to be damaged up into greater focused obligations. Those duties also can be divided time and again in case you need them to.

For an example in this, when you have a undertaking to artwork, then this shape of artwork may be broken down. The smaller works can be:

•Discuss at the side of your colleagues approximately the undertaking

•Do the records analysis that is wanted for the handiest implementation of the venture

•Make the presentation related to the task

•Make the progress file

•Evaluate the assignment implementation

•Some different works that you need to do to finish the task in reality

When you've got were given a take a look at it deeper, that speak with colleagues additionally may be broken down over again to subjects which include:

•Planning the meeting

•Creating the dialogue factors

•Inviting the colleagues and special folks that is probably critical

•Other sports that might make the speak produce the extremely good outcomes.